ALPHA MONEY STRATEGIES

Alpha Male Strategies

ISBN: 978-1070812052

Disclaimer

The reason I wrote this book is because I'm well aware that many young men, particularly young black men, have no financial understanding whatsoever. I'm also aware that a lot of older men have no financial understanding whatsoever. Even me—I didn't even know how a credit score was calculated six short years ago.

That's when I took it upon myself to learn everything I could about money. Having such a large social media influence, I've decided to use that influence for more than just helping men attract women. I want to teach men who are financially ignorant the basics to acquiring financial freedom, as I have. Even if you know a lot about finances, I'm convinced nobody knows it all, so I'm sure I'll make you look at something differently than you previously thought, or at the very minimum, you'll benefit from the mental freedom portion.

I've never claimed to be some financial guru, nor do I want to be. I'm a life and dating coach first and foremost. This book is basically what I've done to change my financial situation around to create financial and mental peace, so take from it what you want, but I'm by no means a financial expert or therapist.

Always consult your financial advisor before investing. If you're having serious mental issues, please consult a professional mental expert. This book is not to advise anyone financially or diagnose any mental disabilities but simply to show you how I turned my life around to becoming a successful entrepreneur.

Table of Contents

What Is Financial Freedom?

You can ask ten people what their definition of financial freedom is, and you'll probably get ten different answers, but for me obtaining financial freedom simply means the amount of money you make passively from investments is more than enough for you to live on, and you're able to live life on your terms.

For example, if you calculate your monthly living expenses as $5,000 a month, and you make $6,000 a month from your investments, then you've obtained financial freedom. These investments could be a business, real estate, stocks, etc. If the investment is a business, then you have to have it where the business pretty much runs itself, without you being involved. If it's a business where it needs your constant attention, then that's not financial freedom in my book. Those monthly expenses have to include everything like bills, food, entertainment, and whatever else you spend money on throughout the month.

When I say you're able to live life on your own terms, I'm simply implying that you've gotten your financial situation to a point where you work when you want to, you can travel anytime you want to, and or you could survive during a financial downfall living a comfortable lifestyle if you had to. By a comfortable lifestyle, I'm referring to not living out of your car, eating bologna sandwiches every day.

Some individuals might imply that it doesn't matter if you live out of car and eat bologna sandwiches every day, as long as you're your own man, and you're on your own schedule. But to me this is not financial freedom because by that indication, a homeless man technically has financial freedom.

That's why I said you could ask ten people their definition of financial freedom, and you would probably get ten different answers.

To me financial freedom can't just mean you have control of your schedule and don't answer to a boss or supervisor. It also has to meet a certain level of living that I'm accustomed to. This doesn't mean I need a T-bone steak and potatoes every night. I do however believe the basic necessities of a nice warm bed, a well-balanced meal three times a day, a hot shower, and, of course, the occasional disposable income to enjoy certain activities I partake in. These activities include—but are not limited to—dining out, traveling, and the occasional night out with the fellas. By my standards, financial freedom isn't freedom if you can't afford to do the things you enjoy doing.

To be fair, though, if the activities you enjoy doing are for the most part free, like, say, fishing, painting, dancing, etc., then I guess you could make a case for a great argument. Unfortunately for me, though, the things I enjoy do require a small amount of disposable income.

With that said, how can one maintain the lifestyle they desire, while simultaneously living life on their own terms? Well that answer is simple. You have to learn how to generate your own income, preferably while you sleep. You heard me right. I said earn money while you sleep, or, as it's commonly known, *passive* or *residual income*.

Passive income is the holy grail to obtaining financial freedom, and is, quite frankly, the only way to truly obtain the financial freedom you're seeking, unless the hobbies and activities you engage in are relatively free. Obtaining this financial freedom will be no small feat, as it requires you achieving certain steps along the way.

First, you have to obtain a skill or education to earn a decent income. That decent income is required because it allows you to have money to invest and pay your bills. This means you'll have to develop the discipline that's needed to live below your means, so you have money to invest. This is called delayed gratification.

After years of investing and acquiring several streams of passive income, you now have achieved the financial freedom you've been seeking. It takes several years of investing to have enough passive income coming in to maintain your lifestyle if you no longer had active income coming in. Active income is when you trade time for money. In my opinion, downgrading your lifestyle is not financial freedom unless you were living some overextravagant lifestyle that should have been downgraded long ago anyway.

What is Mental Peace?

Most individuals place great value on obtaining financial freedom but rarely think about obtaining the all-important mental peace. Some might say the two are directly related and, in some cases, this might actually be true. But in my opinion, they differ in one unique way.

Mental peace, most of the time comes, from who or what you allow in your life and not living beyond your means. This can be certain family members, friends, a toxic work environment, spouse or lover, business associates, and or even neighbors. You can never expect to achieve mental peace if you continue to allow toxic and negative people into your life, or you're obsessed with trying to impress others by living beyond your means. Mental peace is achieved when your stress level is at a relatively low level.

I don't know if it's possible to ever get it to a complete zero, but coming pretty close to that is obtainable. Life is a rollercoaster of sorts, so there will always be things that have us stressed or peeved at times. I don't think it's possible to obtain mental peace without obtaining some level of financial freedom, but mental peace requires obtaining financial freedom and disposing of toxic negative people from your life.

This is why this is so much harder to obtain because the average person simply can't rid themselves of toxic individuals out of the fear of being alone. A scarcity mind-set is a detriment in life. It's a detriment with your finances as it prevents you from investing out of a fear of loss. It's the same situation with allowing toxic individuals in your life who add little to no value to your life. You can't expect to obtain any sense of financial or mental freedom when you have a fear of loss or a scarcity mind-set.

Make a promise to yourself right now. From this day forward, you will no longer allow negative individuals to zap your positive energy with their negativity, no matter who they are.

Find Your Purpose

Anybody who is remotely familiar with my work knows that one of the biggest things I preach is that everyone should find what their purpose and mission in life is. This is the cornerstone to happiness in life. When you have a purpose in life, you no longer have time for toxic individuals.

We all have to work to provide a living for ourselves. So let's assume the typical person's workday is eight hours long, eight hours sleeping, that still leaves eight hours unaccounted for.

I wanted to point this out first, before all the "I don't have time to work on my purpose" people chimed in. This is usually where people have a void that needs filling. Most people try to fill this void with finding a significant other. The problem with this is that you can come across needy. When I'm referring to being needy, I'm not just referring to the opposite sex. I'm also referring to friendships also. Needy friends are as off-putting as a needy lover. Feeling lonely is the breeding ground of neediness, so it's counterproductive to hope to fill that void with someone because your neediness would probably only turn them off eventually anyway.

There's only one thing that fills this void and makes you more attractive at the same time by making you more unavailable, and that's pursuing your purpose. Finding your purpose could literally take years and could change from time to time. As we age and mature, our interest can—and will, more times than not—change. I was once obsessed with fitness, but that passion dimmed over time as I became more fascinated with being a life coach and YouTube personality. That passion is now giving way to becoming a great author. I can't speak for everyone, but I like change every so often, as it's a challenge for me to tackle a different activity.

One thing that keeps coming up is that people will say, "I can't find my purpose." People will say this, but they never think to step out of their comfort zone. One characteristic of many people is that they hate stepping out of their comfort zone. If you're having trouble finding your purpose, try a variety of things. When trying different things, you're bound to find something you have a passion for.

This is a rare scenario though. Most people know what they have a passion for. The problem is social programming. We have been programmed all our lives to go to school so we can build a resume to work for someone else. Funny thing is, whoever you're working for, decided at some point that they weren't going to be an employee for someone else.

We have been told all our lives that the key to success is education and employment. You rarely hear society encourage entrepreneurship. People work their entire lives paralyzed in fear of unemployment. I say this not to encourage you to quit your job. I say this to let you know that if others did it, then you can too. Finding or getting on your purpose doesn't mean you can quit your job tomorrow. You have to look at it as if you have two jobs. It could take years before your purpose is actually making money.

With that being said your purpose should be something you not only enjoy but have a passion for. If you're having a hard time staying focused on your purpose, then it's probably not your purpose.

A common mistake I see when it comes down to purpose is people confuse doing something that'll pay them well with something that they actually enjoy and have a passion for. People will say they want to be a lawyer. They usually don't have a passion for law. They just know most lawyers typically make a nice salary, which is true, but it'll do nothing to make you happy.

What I've found in life is that money does little to actually make you happy. Don't get me wrong; there's nothing wrong with making money, but the key to happiness is making money doing what you genuinely love to do. Just think of all the famous rich celebrities you know who aren't happy. People will have something they have a genuine interest for, but they think, "There's no way I can make a living doing that." This is what usually holds people back from pursuing their purpose.

People put limits on themselves due to social programming reinforcing the slave—my mistake—employee mind-set. Let me be clear, there's nothing wrong with having a job, but if you have that job due to your fear of failure, then that's a problem.

Grind Phase

There's a grind phase you must go through to see your purpose to fruition. The grind phase is usually when the average person gives up due to the amount of commitment they're putting in, without seeing much initial return on investment. Yes, investing your time, even if you're not spending money, is an investment because time is the biggest asset you have to invest.

You typically will have your nine-to-five job, and in your spare time, you're working on your purpose. This usually means you can expect virtually little to no social life for approximately a year or longer.

This unwillingness to sacrifice or delay gratification is what leads people to a life of mediocrity. To accomplish anything in life, it's going to require some type of sacrifice. People who aren't willing to sacrifice end up working for an employer who was willing to sacrifice.

The social aspect isn't the only deterrent to focusing on your purpose. One of the hardest aspects of working and building up your purpose is that you'll spend hours working on something that doesn't even pay you anything. In some cases, this will require you to cut down on, or in some instances give up, some of the income you're making now for something that isn't bringing anything in at the moment. This means downgrading your lifestyle now for a much better lifestyle later. These downgrades may include not buying the latest outfit, not going out for dinner, not dating as much, getting a smaller apartment, or even getting a roommate, etc.

People are willing to make this sacrifice for a short period of time but give up if they don't see things starting to take off as fast as they hoped things would pick up. The reason they do this is because they're pursuing their purpose for money, which is the wrong reason. Pursuing your purpose, your primary reason, should always be happiness and self-fulfillment first and foremost—not finances.

As most of you probably know, pursuing your purpose is also the key to being successful in dating and relationships. When you're pursuing your purpose, this leaves you unavailable, which is highly attractive to both sexes, as long as it's within reason. You can't be so unavailable that the person you're dating never sees you. Anyone would lose interest in that case.

Balance is key, so you have to make yourself somewhat available if you want to keep someone interested. So, just by chance, when you're pursuing your purpose in life, you improve your financial situation and dating life.

Monetization of Purpose

The hardest part, for the majority of people, is that once you've figured out your purpose, how do you monetize it? For me, this was the easiest part. Thanks to social media, it has never been easier to monetize your passion in life.

If you're a musician or writer, most record companies or publishers won't even sign you unless you have a social media following. The reason they do this is because they know you'll already have a fan base to sell to. The reason this information is so important is because it doesn't matter how good your products or services are, you must have a following or customer base to purchase your product or service.

My suggestion to everyone reading this book is to start building a social media following. That's YouTube, Facebook, Instagram, Snapchat, Twitter, etc. It will likely take you several months, if not years, before you're ready to monetize your purpose. In the meantime, you can simultaneously build your social media following.

When I'm referencing years to sell your product or service, I'm talking about the amount of time it's likely to take you to refine your skill or product. See, when I became a personal trainer, I was good at it because I had been working out and studying the fitness industry for several years by that point in my life. It took me years to learn the body. When I became a dating and life coach on YouTube, I had dated hundreds, and possibly thousands, of women by that point. It took me years of dating to acquire that knowledge through trial and error. So it didn't happen overnight.

You should post as often as you can. YouTube is probably the best platform, as it actually pays you to post once your channel is monetized. Other platforms are actually moving in this direction as well. The thing with YouTube is that it allows you to build more of a connection with your following, as opposed to the other social media platforms.

Besides, Google is king. I know for a fact that whenever I don't understand something, I google how to do it. This is where properly tagging your videos comes into play. When someone googles how to do something, if your video is tagged properly, your video should pop up.

What I've learned from having my own YouTube channel is that it's not so much about the quality of equipment you're using, but rather the delivery and quality of information you're relaying. So before you go out and purchase ten thousand dollars' worth of video equipment, just keep in mind that it won't mean a hill of beans if your delivery and the quality of your content—and by content, I mean message—isn't up to par. I know plenty of high-quality equipment channels with less than stellar views than, say, a channel like the Hodgetwins, which is basically a couple of guys recording with their camera phone.

Being likable online is also important because people have a tendency to buy products from people whom they genuinely like, so playing the villain online might not be the smartest move if you have plans to sell a product or service in the future.

Patience is a virtue when you're on your purpose and building a social media following. Nothing happens overnight, so you shouldn't expect to build a multimillion-dollar business overnight. You will have to start with zero followers just like everyone else.

Hopefully, after about a year or so, you can start to promote your product or service online, if it's ready to do so. If not, then just be patient. It's better to wait a little longer than to put out a half-assed product before you're supposed to.

If this is your first product or service you've put out, it can be a daunting task to recover from putting out low-quality work initially. Ideally, you would like to never put out low-quality material, but what you think is good and what the consumer thinks is good may be two different things. If you have a proven track record, it'll be easier to recover from a less-than-stellar product.

For example, if Stephen King puts out a poor book, it'll be a little easier for him to recover from given his track record of putting out excellent books. On the other hand, if I put out a low-quality book, it'll be much harder for me to get the consumer to purchase my next book due to my short track record.

When you're putting out a product or service, there has to be a trust factor with the consumer that you'll give them their money worth, since, in most cases, they won't be able to get their money back, or at the very least be a hassle they aren't willing to deal with. Once that trust is lost you lose support in the future products or services you're offering.

In today's social media age, where people can communicate via the internet, it is more important than ever to put out quality material or services, thanks to product and service reviews everywhere you turn. Everything on Amazon gets ratings and reviews. With that being said, once you've figured out what your purpose is, make sure you built a strong following on social media to sell product or services to.

Once you've figured out your purpose and built your following, it's time to figure out how you're going to present your product or service to the consumer. I prefer to sell a product or service that reaches multiple individuals at once, as opposed to one individual at a time.

This means you want to create a program, subscription service, or self-help book, if you're selling knowledge. You want to avoid consultations if possible, because at that point, you're selling your time. Nothing wrong with consultations, but you want the overwhelming majority of your time spent building something that creates passive income.

It's very hard to create financial freedom with active income. I'm not saying it's impossible, but it's definitely harder. Remember your time is the most precious thing you have.

Obviously, if you're selling merchandise or a patented product, you obviously want to let your following know you have products for sale. Don't oversell your product, though, as this will turn most of your following off as you'll appear to be a greedy vendor, constantly throwing merchandise in their face. A good rule of thumb is to just put your website in your videos at the bottom of the screen without talking about it that often. Maybe once a week you mention in your videos to your followers where they can go to find your products.

If you do offer consultations, make sure you charge accordingly. The vast majority of your business should be selling a product, not consultations. If you're a musician, comedian, or any kind of other entertainer, you obviously want an album or recorded act to sell to your following. If you're offering a service, you want employees or independent contractors providing the service, not you.

You should spend your time trying to grow your following and the products you're offering. Selling your time for money is shortsighted and not seeing the big picture. You have to think big to get your business big. I know it seems smart to provide the service yourself, as you'll be able to keep all the money since you're not paying anyone, but it actually inhibits you from growing your business efficiently. Successful people think, "How is this going to benefit me twenty years from now?" Poor people think, "How is this going to affect me today?"

Law of Attraction

I'm a big proponent in the law of attraction. There are different interpretations of the law of attraction, but what it means to me is that you get the same energy back that you put out. You reap what you sow, so to speak.

You can't expect to build a multimillion-dollar business working ten hours a week. You can't expect to meet the woman of your dreams if you're afraid to approach women (whether using a cold approach or choosing signals) or not presenting the best version of yourself. Most men are single due to the fact they're afraid to open their mouth. The only shots you miss are the ones you never take.

You can't expect to build a company or attract the woman of your dreams if you genuinely don't believe you're able to obtain what you are seeking. I don't believe in luck or coincidences, but what I do believe in is that when you put yourself in position by simply striving to obtain your goals, things just seem to fall in your lap. That's not luck; that's the universe's way of making things happen when you put the time and energy in.

When I first arrived in New York I had no job waiting for me, but I knew that if I got out every morning looking for a job, something would come through. And sure enough, within two weeks, I had found a job. This, I remind you, was during the Great Recession.

Let's say you're trying to sell a product that you've created, and now you're out trying to convince stores to carry your product or give you shelf space. Well, if you grind it long enough, what will probably happen along the way is that you'll probably meet someone who either carries your product or offers you something even better, like licensing. Maybe you meet someone who offers you something you weren't even pursuing. Who knows?

All I know is that things seem to just happen when you put yourself out there. The thing is, you probably won't even meet the person who is destined to change your life in a store, but rather on a train or at a Starbucks. That's how the law of attraction works.

Most people would chalk this up to luck, but I don't believe in luck. I call this an opportunity that you created through hard work and perseverance.

The same can be said about meeting the woman of your dreams. When you're actively looking for a wife via internet dating or clubs, it seems like you never can find the woman of your dreams. That's because you're sending desperate energy into the universe, and it can come across as needy when you do find someone you're truly into.

On the other hand, if you're on your purpose in life and have an active social life, you'll project the right energy into the universe and come across as complete, which will naturally make you more attractive since you're not desperate for a relationship. Another thing to consider is that when you're living an active social life, once again, luck will rear its head again when you meet the woman of your dreams at a gas station pumping gas. It wouldn't even be possible to meet this woman sitting in your house playing World of Warcraft. Opportunities always seem abundant when you're putting positive energy and actions into the world.

Don't count on getting lucky. Create your own luck by putting the work in. Trying to sell a product is a lot like approaching women. You have to genuinely believe what you're selling in your heart. Consumers are just like women in that they can tell when you truly believe in what you're selling. You have to truly believe that your product or service is going to bring value to the consumer.

When a salesman tries to sell me a product, I can tell from his body language and tone if he truly believes in what he's selling. Women have this innate ability when you approach them. In the real world, we call this confidence. To get this confidence you need to really believe in what you're putting out.

This is why it's important to leave no rock unturned when you're on your purpose. Make sure you give your purpose everything you've got. Therefore, when it's time to monetize your purpose, you genuinely, in your heart, believe in what you are selling.

Life Is about Choices

Growing up in Alabama, I was always taught you have your haves and have nots. Unfortunately for me, no one ever explained why you have the haves and have nots.

Having an understanding of the world as I do today, it's quite easy for me to see why you have a separation in social classes. Everyone has the same twenty-four hours in the day, so how are there millionaires and billionaires on one hand, and on the other hand, you have people who are struggling to keep a roof over their head? Well the answer is quite simple—*choices* or *decisions*.

See, what I've learned about life is it basically boils down to the *choices* you make. Low- and middle-class people make choices that give them short-term gratification. Rich and wealthy people make choices that give them long-term gratification. It's just that simple.

Low-income people are individuals who typically have no skill, trade, or education. Therefore, they tend to work manual or low-paying labor jobs that require very little skill, if any skill at all. These jobs typically pay minimum wage or slightly above. This low income forces the individual to focus on keeping a roof over their heads or keeping the lights on, and understandably so.

Now, here is where *choice* comes into play. I once was a part of the lower class, working as a bouncer in Manhattan for approximately thirty grand a year. Keep in mind that I'm now located in New York, so thirty grand a year doesn't go as far here as it would most other states. I made a *choice* that I didn't want to be a part of the lower class anymore, so I got certified as a personal trainer.

I could have kept the victim mentality and stayed a bouncer, making thirty grand a year, complaining, or I could have been sick and tired of being sick and tired and decide to get a high-paying skill. Obviously, I chose the latter.

The key to escaping the lower class is a skill or an education. There's no way around it. Maybe you get lucky and get a job that pays middle-class income with no skill, but I would then ask you, What if you lost that job? How confident are you in getting that same kind of opportunity again? A skill or education allows you to have something you can always fall back on. No one can take that knowledge you've obtained. What are the odds that happens again?

The middle class is where most working individuals find themselves. These are typically individuals who have some sort of skill and or education.

Here's where most middle-class individuals go wrong, however. Although they have the income to invest, they *choose* to buy liabilities. Liabilities are anything that require some sort of risk, as in loans or acquiring something that depreciates in value over time. Examples of these would be cars, electronics, etc. A good rule of thumb is if it has tires, it's a liability.

If you *choose* to buy liabilities with your excess income, then you're destined to stay in the rat race forever. The rat race is when you trade time for money. There are only so many hours in a day. Hence, why trading time for money will never lead to financial wealth.

Delayed gratification is the name of the game when it comes to acquiring wealth. The secret is to invest in assets. Assets are things that tend to appreciate in value over time or make you money.

In other words, if you buy wall art and it just maintains its value then technically it's a liability. The reason for this is because if it doesn't appreciate to at least keep up with inflation, then it's a liability. If you paid $10,000 for a picture today, and you decided to sell this particular picture ten years from now, and you were only able to sell it for the same price you paid for it, then you took a loss. That $10,000 doesn't go as far as it did when you bought it ten years ago, thanks to inflation.

Due to this fact, there aren't many things you buy that aren't an asset or a liability. Something is usually either appreciating or depreciating. The rich buy liabilities just like everyone else, but the only difference is that they tend to buy their liabilities or toys with returns on investments (ROIs). Rich people invest their money into things like real estate, stocks, bonds, or their business, and then they take the profits from their investment to buy their liabilities.

We've all watched *Lifestyles of the Rich and Famous* and *Cribs* on MTV. We know wealthy people have no shortage of toys. Middle-class individuals take their income and buy their toys trying to look rich. Some middle-class individuals even go as far as to acquire debt to achieve this false sense of wealth.

I teach individuals to pursue their passion and purpose. If done correctly, eventually some financial success should come from that. If so, you're going to have to make a choice somewhere down the road. Do you want to buy things (liabilities) to look rich, or are you willing to have a little delayed gratification, so later you can take that money and invest it to where your money is working for you and you no longer have to work for money?

This is commonly referred to as letting your money work for you. You have to take on the mind-set that your money is like employees, and they work for you. A lot of rich people don't even have employees because they invest their money so well.

If you have five thousand dollars to spend, a better way to look at it is to say to yourself, "I have five thousand employees working for me," and not "I have five thousand dollars to spend on worthless crap." You have to rid yourself of that instant gratification mind-set if you ever hope to acquire any real financial success.

What Should Be Your First Investment

Life is pretty simple, unfortunately most people make it more difficult than it should be. I can tell you from experience that if you don't acquire some type of education, skill, or trade in your lifetime, you're more than likely going to have a much more difficult time in life.

Therefore, your first investment should be in yourself. Your active income will usually be your biggest moneymaker. Investing is just a better alternative to saving your money, or even worse, buying liabilities. When you learn a skill or acquire an education, you're making the biggest and smartest investment in your life, in my opinion.

I have a personal trainer certification, and no matter what happens throughout my lifetime, you can never take that knowledge from me. I've made back that $500 I invested in that certification several times over. The world is built on what value you can bring to a company or marketplace. If you work a low-paying, non-skilled job in life, then you bring very low value to the job market. A good rule of thumb is if it only took you a couple of hours of on-the-job training, you're not likely to be compensated very well financially for services rendered.

I worked mediocre jobs all my life due to not taking life seriously enough in my younger years. I primarily teach entrepreneurship these days, but it takes most people many years to discover their passion and purpose. Having a skill or education can help you live a fruitful life until you discover what it is you have a passion for. Even if you are one of the lucky ones to discover their passion in life at an early age, you're not likely to make a living doing it, initially. It usually takes years of honing your skills before that happens.

There's an important saying in the real world: The harder you work, the less you make. I can tell you that throughout my life, I've found this to be true. If you're younger, I hope my words are coming through. In fact, even if you're an older person, because it's never too late to change your life around, but I expect an older person to already know this.

I didn't get a skill until I was thirty-four years old. Up until that point in my life, I worked one mediocre job after another. I remember vividly of complaining to my security job supervisor about getting a raise. I had been there for nearly four years and had never gotten or asked for a raise.

Need I remind you, but as most of you know, the cost of living goes up every year due to inflation. So that means if you're working a job that doesn't give raises often, you're essentially making less money each year due to inflation. In other words, your dollar loses value each year.

When I would ask the manager for the raise, he would agree, but months would pass, and nothing would happen. I would ask again every couple of months, basically begging at this point. You shouldn't have to be on your hands and knees begging someone for a raise. If they value what you bring to their business, it shouldn't be a problem. Anytime you ask someone more than once for something, you're basically begging at that point.

Anyway, getting back to the story, every time I would ask for a raise, he would agree. After about the fourth or fifth time of asking, I remember saying to myself, you know what, it's not his responsibility to get me more money. It's my own responsibility to get me more money.

I had been a personal trainer for years but mostly as a side hustle. A client here and there, but I never really took it seriously, and I had no certification or anything like that. You will have life-altering situations that send your life in a totally different path.

I had one of these encounters with a club patron at the club where I was providing security a few months before I started asking the club manager for a raise. I remember it like yesterday. It was this French guy in the club who approached me and asked me how I got so big. He came to the club early when it was dead, so I guess he was just trying to pass time. Little did I know, this conversation would change my life. After about an hour of breaking down my diet and workout program, the guy said something that insulted and inspired me at the same time. He said, "You should think about doing that for a living instead of standing by this door as a security guard."

I'm not going to lie. At first, I was furious. I took it as an insult that the guy was basically saying that I had a crappy job. I spent most of that night feeling angry and sorry for myself. Later that night on my way home, I vowed to do what the French guy recommended, and that was to go in full pursuit of my passion.

The very next day I contacted NASM to inquire about the cost of certification. I didn't have a lot of money, so luckily for me they offered a monthly payment plan. I ordered the study material for the certification, and I can still remember the euphoria I felt, finally pursuing my passion for a living. I couldn't afford to quit my job just yet, and most likely, you won't either once you discover your purpose.

I worked the security job at night and studied the personal training certification material in the daytime. It was much harder than I initially thought it would be, given my training history, but I quickly found out that I had more to learn than I initially thought. But I was determined to turn my life around.

After about six months of studying, I took the test and passed it on the first try. I was ecstatic. I was officially a skilled worker. The certification takes a couple of weeks to send through the mail, but that didn't stop me from going out and inquiring about training jobs the very next day. Believe it or not, I got an interview the very first day I went out looking for a training job.

That's a little of that law of attraction working for me right there. What I mean is that when I left the house, I knew in my heart I would get a job, or at least an interview. I believed in my ability to convince anybody interviewing me that there was not a trainer alive that would outwork me.

See, there will always be someone more skilled than you, and I'm fine with that because I know it's a process, but I refuse to be outworked by anyone. I virtually lived in the gym to build my clientele. This is why it's essential to pursue something you have a genuine passion for. That way working a one-hundred-hour workweek never feels like work.

I initially thought I would train in the daytime and do security at night, but once I started working at the gym training, I knew I would have to give it all of my attention if I wanted to build my business. This is a decision we all must make at some point, once you decide to pursue your purpose.

I had no savings due to living from check to check. Working a skilled position increased my income tenfold. See, the reason my income increased so dramatically was because I now had acquired a valuable skill that I could demand a higher fee for. Putting it simply, I brought more value to the marketplace.

When you're working an unskilled position, you don't have this same leverage since your boss can simply replace you by lunchtime. Now, personal trainers come a dime a dozen, but a good trainer is rare. This is what makes you valuable. Don't let this confuse you with being irreplaceable because every employee is replaceable. Perfecting your skill allows you to put a higher price on your skill set.

This is why it's not time to rest on your laurels once you've acquired a skill set. You have to grind just as hard to develop your skill to differentiate yourself from others in your profession.

Conquering Your Fear of Failure

Perhaps the biggest hurdle to overcome, once you've discovered your purpose, is your fear of failure. It's easy to have this fear when you're constantly reminded of how many businesses fail their first year. This is the social programming that keeps people in fear of being their own boss.

What they don't tell you is that most of those businesses fail due to the lack of due diligence and patience it takes to build a successful business. Most people start businesses with the mind-set that they'll be able to work less as their own boss. That's the wrong mind-set to have when starting a business. There's nothing wrong with having that to be a goal in the long term, but unfortunately you work more, not less, when starting a business.

That's not even the worst part. The worst part is despite all this time and financial investment, there's usually very little return on investment in the beginning. This lack of fast return on investment is what causes people to give up.

Developing a long-term mind-set is the hardest thing to develop if you've been raised to be an employee and consumer all your life. The average person that starts a business doesn't have the ability to have delayed gratification. You must have the ability to sacrifice your desire for superficial material things and an abundant social life to build a successful business. There's no way around it.

When I started my YouTube channel, it took them seven months to monetize my channel. That didn't stop me from making at least four videos a week, all the while still personal training my clients in the morning while simultaneously running my security company. Oh, did I mention I was writing my first book at the same time? I didn't mind because I knew it would all pay off in the end. I said all that to say this one important thing: be prepared to get very little return on your investment in the beginning of opening any business.

When I was thirty-three years old, I had the biggest epiphany of my life. I realized the biggest issue I had always had in my life was a fear of stepping out of my comfort zone. I realized that I had been a failure due to the fact I had never failed. All my life, I worked minimally skilled jobs that required no skill—or brains, for that matter. I protected myself from failure this way.

This fear of failure all but guarantees you a life of mediocrity. You must fail to succeed. Think of all the great inventions in the world. Do you think they got it right the first try? It more than likely took many failures to finally get it right.

The personal trainer I had in my midtwenties for about a month would always tell me that soreness is weakness leaving the body. Well, you have to look at failures the same way. Failure just means success is right around the corner, if you're willing to persevere.

When we see successful people on TV, we subconsciously think to ourselves, "That could never be me." In fact, the only difference between you and that person is that they had the wherewithal to not let a fear of failure hold them back from pursuing their dreams and passion. All those celebrities, with a few exceptions of nepotism, were once regular individuals, just like you, and had to bust their behinds to get where they are. They're made of flesh and bone just like you and me.

Jay-Z had a very good line in his song "Can I Live" where he raps, "I'll rather die enormous than live dormant." This basically means he'd rather die pursuing what he wants than live in fear of failure. You can't expect to be successful until you lose your fear of failure.

Don't Be Afraid to Relocate

Being from a small town, I'll be the first one to admit that living in a small town does limit your options as an entrepreneur. Beyond that, you don't get a lot of inspiration from your surroundings. Where I'm from, everyone I know has a *job*.

The only person I know individually who had an entrepreneurial spirit was my uncle. He was a self-employed shade tree mechanic. I guess that's where I got my entrepreneurial spirit from without even knowing it. I always felt I was destined to be my own boss.

This came at a cost though. I had five different jobs a year because I would constantly quit or get fired due to the fact that I didn't think the job I was doing was up to par for what I wanted, despite having no college degrees or skills. I now know I was quitting those jobs due to not having a passion for what I was doing, but my family and friends thought I was quitting jobs due to laziness, which couldn't be the further from the truth. I just had this deep down feeling I wasn't living up to my full potential. Being from a small town, I really didn't feel inspired to be an entrepreneur. I just didn't want to work a subpar job.

This life of mediocrity would continue throughout my twenties. When I was thirty years old, a female acquaintance asked me to create a Facebook account, and I obliged. Little did I know, creating that account would change my life forever.

Once on Facebook, I ended up befriending a female by the name of Tiffany. Tiffany lived in New York. We would carry on a long-distance relationship for almost a year. She would travel back and forth to see me about once every other month. As you can imagine, this got old over time, as it was a big investment on her part not to mention we both wanted to see each other more as we got closer.

We ultimately decided that it was best if one of us relocated. She suggested I move to New York. This was not a hard sell due to the fact I wanted a fresh start anyway. I would be lying if I omitted the fact that there were signs Tiffany and I wouldn't exactly be a match made in heaven, due to the fact of how much masculine energy Tiffany carried. Having a lot of masculine energy myself, we literally disagreed on everything. I now know this was probably due to her having a low attraction level to me, but I wasn't aware of this at the time. I was willing to overlook this, however, as I saw this as an opportunity to escape the gerbil wheel of Alabama.

I knew Tiffany and I probably wouldn't last long due to her dominant personality. I knew when I left Alabama that I would have to hit the ground running so I would at least have employment in the event of a future breakup. Driving out of Alabama, I felt this weight being lifted off my shoulders.

Most of the jobs in Alabama are temporary jobs with no benefits or job security. I no longer had to deal with mediocre job after mediocre job. Most of the companies back home liked the convenience of not having to go through the hiring process when adding employees. It's much easier for them to just call a temp service and have them send them another disposable employee.

I would now take New York by storm. I'm not saying you need to get online and befriend someone from a big town with the hopes of relocating. What I am saying is that relocating is definitely something you should consider, if given the opportunity. Maybe you aren't given the opportunity to relocate from meeting a girl on Facebook. You might have to just do it the old-fashioned way. That's working and saving as much as you can so you can relocate.

Once I reached New York, I felt rejuvenated. Seeing all the immigrant entrepreneurs really inspired me to be my own boss one day. There was literally an immigrant entrepreneur on every corner selling some type of product or food. Whether it was Chinese food or hair shops or bodegas. I don't see how any American-born citizen doesn't get some kind of entrepreneur inspiration seeing so many immigrant entrepreneurs.

I'm a big proponent of the theory that we are a product of our environment. The only reason I could imagine for American citizens living in New York to not have some kind of entrepreneurial spirit is the fear of failure. Being an employee is a lot safer than being your own boss. Now, don't get me wrong. Don't expect that moving to a big city will fix your problems. It doesn't matter where you move, if you don't change your mind-set or be open to change, your life won't change much. As with anything in life, you get what you put in.

Do What You Have to Do

Once I got to New York, I only had about four thousand dollars to my name. That was from the sale of my furniture to my best friend before leaving. That's nothing when you consider the fact that I had to pay bills in a city as expensive as New York. I had no income yet, so I was basically living off my life savings.

Having dreams is one thing, but I also had bills and was fully aware of how finances cause rifts in relationships. I left home every morning before eight a.m. and treated my job search like a nine-to five-job. I was well aware of the law of attraction and knew something would come through if I was willing to put the work in. I even applied to minimum wage jobs. Something was better than nothing, right? I knew my savings wouldn't last long if I didn't get some kind of income quickly. I was even trying to enroll in a trade school to finally get a skill.

During the enrollment process, I met an individual who just so happened to have a cousin with his own security company (law of attraction). What are the chances of that happening? Here I am, this six-foot, four-inch, three hundred-plus pound powerlifter, perfect for security, and this guy just so happens to have a cousin with a security company.

Security doesn't pay well by New York standards, but it would at least have money coming in until I figured my next move. I didn't move all the way from Alabama to New York to be a security guard, but dreams don't pay any bills.

If you want to be successful in life you can't be afraid to do what you have to do until you can achieve what you want to achieve. I would soon forget about the vision I had when I left Alabama and fell right back into the trap of short-term thinking.

This is how many individuals end up working subpar jobs all their life. They get comfortable with their current situation. I had changed locations, but I hadn't fully changed my short-term mind-set. At the end of the day, you can relocate to anywhere in the world you want, but until you have a complete mind overhaul, it doesn't mean much.

Before long I was working all the overtime I could handle at the club. What I should have done was work the security job at night and went to trade school in the daytime. Looking back at it now, it might be a blessing that I didn't go to trade school because maybe I wouldn't have ever pursued my true passion, which was working out, but that wasn't the initial reason I didn't pursue a skill.

Short-term thinking means you want all your return up front. Long-term thinking simply means you don't mind forgoing an initial return on investment in the hopes of getting a bigger return in the future. I was still in the short-term thinking phase. Getting a skill meant putting in work for something that wouldn't give me a return for many months in advance.

I hated my security job, not to mention it was a graveyard shift job. Tiffany and I were done at this point, and my family was over a thousand miles away, so I had no support system to fall back on. I knew what I had a passion for, but I hadn't figured out what my purpose in life was. I knew I would have to be a security guard in the meantime until I figured it out.

Don't quit jobs or school on a pipe dream. Do what you have to do until you find out what your life purpose is. That's called being a responsible adult.

Multiple Passions

A common occurrence that happens when most individuals decide to pursue their passion in life is that they can't decide which passion they should pursue. For example, let's use Bo Jackson. He was a very good football player, but he also had a passion for baseball, although he wasn't as good in my opinion. The same could be said for Deion Sanders.

I don't believe that it's wise to pursue two or more passions. I firmly believe that it's best to pick one and pursue whichever one you have the most passion for. An argument could be made that you should pursue what you're naturally better at. I feel you should pursue what you have more of a passion for, because I believe that if you want to be successful at something, you have to give it your all.

Let's not forget all the enjoyment you get from pursuing something that you're 100 percent passionate about. I don't think you can expect to become the best at what you're trying to accomplish with half effort. To fully maximize your potential, it's going to take all the energy you have to really get it where you're trying to take it.

In football, they have a saying that if you have two quarterbacks, you have none. That's because when you use two quarterbacks, you don't allow one quarterback to get a feel for the game. Pursuing your purpose is the same way: you kind of develop a feel as you go along for what you need to do next. You develop a schedule and you learn to stick to it.

After coming to grips that you need to pick one passion and pursue that, you're stuck with the almighty decision of deciding which passion will that be. A good way to decide is by asking yourself, which one would I do for absolutely free? If you're willing to do something for absolutely free, that's a pretty good way of gauging genuine passion. The reason this is important is that it's a very good chance your passion will take a while to get going. If that's the case, you won't give up quickly because you're not making money initially, because it's likely you won't.

If you try to base this decision for financial reasons, it's highly likely that when things get difficult or hit a snag, you'll likely just quit and go back into the workforce. I know it's not easy to say goodbye to a passion of yours, but it's going to be nearly impossible to get your business where you want to get it if you're pursuing two passions. Realistically, you need to work sixteen-hour days if you want your passion to take off. There won't even be much time to maintain a social life, never mind pursuing a second passion.

If there's a way you could combine the two passions, then that would be even better. Take myself, for instance. I have a passion for fitness and being a life coach. Well, since I preach becoming the best version of yourself, it was very easy for me to combine the two, since fitness is a part of the self-improvement I preach. I don't have time to train clients individually anymore, however, as most of my day is dedicated to being a life coach.

When to Change Passions

For some people, there will come a time where you will lose the passion you once had for your purpose. This happens due to the fact that, as we age, what intrigued us five or ten years ago might not fascinate us anymore. That's just typical human nature.

Now, this loss of passion shouldn't have anything to do with the fact that you aren't making the money you want to make. If that's the case, then your entire motivation to pursue your passion was based solely on financial gain.

Don't get me wrong; I like making money as much as the next person, but if that's the main factor or biggest factor in you pursuing your passion, you're almost always going to fail. Most businesses fail due to not putting in the time and effort to make it succeed. This failure, more times than not, leads the entrepreneur to give up and go back to their nine-to-five.

A wise man once said, "It's better to do what you love for a living, and make very little money, than to be rich doing a job you hate." I've found this to be true in my life. This aside, there's also another reason people want to change directions. You simply discover you have a greater passion for something else than your current passion.

I have firsthand experience with this, as it happened to me. I was once obsessed with fitness, but I soon discovered I had an even greater passion. That passion was teaching men to stop complaining about female nature and to become the best version of themselves. I felt like I would be the perfect guy to teach guys how to attract women, since I had so much experience dating.

It seems like every week, I was going on six to eight dates. Two dates on Friday, two dates on Saturday, and two dates on Sunday. Going on that many dates, you get pretty good at dating. It wasn't long after that I decided to use what I learned from going on so many dates to help other guys who might not have had my success with women.

I made this decision based on the fact that I enjoyed helping guys attract the type of women they deserved more than I enjoyed helping people lose weight. This was more of me burning out on the fitness more than anything. I'm the type of individual who gets bored over time with pretty much anything I've done. Money did not weigh into my decision one bit, as we all know there's plenty of rich fitness gurus. The biggest contributing factor for me was my need for a new challenge.

When you start pursuing your passion, it's fun and exciting because it's challenging to get it to succeed, but once you've seen a level of success, and the challenge is gone, you could lose passion for it.

I remember when I decided to become a personal trainer full-time. I was so pumped to become the best trainer in the city. I literally studied everything about anatomy that I could put my hands on for the next few years. I was determined to become the best trainer in New York City. I know this is a very biased opinion, but in my opinion, I became that. My clients would also express this to me, as most of them had worked with several trainers prior to working out with me.

I soon lost the motivation and passion I once had, as I had accomplished my goal of becoming the best trainer in the city. If you're a competitive person like me, don't be surprised if you lose passion for your purpose once you accomplish a certain level of success. In a situation like that, if you've lost the fire you once had, I think it's perfectly fine to change directions.

Delayed Gratification

Sacrifice is the name of the game to succeed in life. I think it's safe to say that most people like having nice things, and I'm no exception to this. I like nice cars, clothes, jewelry, and a nice living space just as much as the next person, but in order to fulfill your passion sacrifices will have to be made.

If you have nice things now, like a luxury car or apartment, you may have to downgrade your car and or apartment in order to give yourself the time necessary to allow your passion to grow. Pursuing one's passion in life is not an overnight thing. It's going to be hard to keep pursuing your passion if bill collectors are knocking at the front door. You don't want to have to rush things, because this will prevent you from making smart, long-term decisions for short-term financial gains.

I'll give you a prime example with myself. When I first created my YouTube page, Patreon was the new big thing. A lot of creators were moving to Patreon to make money since YouTube had encountered what is now commonly referred to as "The Adpocalypse."

Certain creators in my sector of YouTube chastised me, since I was getting tons of views and subscriptions but very little Patreon support. If guys wanted to support me, they were more than welcome to join my Patreon page, but I wasn't putting content on my Patreon page yet, due to the fact that I knew I needed to build my brand and following more before I started building my Patreon page. Trying to build my Patreon page would have been shortsighted and caused me to lose focus on what was best for me long-term, which of course was building my brand and following.

If I had been pressed for cash, I would have more than likely had no other choice but to cut my brand building short and focus on making some immediate cash by building my Patreon page. The problem with going to Patreon and leaving YouTube is that it doesn't have the same platform that YouTube offers. YouTube is basically Google, for God's sake.

Another example is the movie *Rocky IV*. In that movie, Rocky told his protégé to not sign with the boxing promoter The Duke.

For all those who don't know, boxing promoters take most of the earnings from boxers. They're able to do this the same way most record labels are able to. They usually give the fighter some sort of lump sum payment up front to sign, then very little on the back end. The same can be said for book publishing companies. They know the artist, fighter, or author is so fascinated with the signing bonus that they forgo all the money on the back end.

Boxing promoters, record labels and book publishing companies have been taking advantage of shortsighted individuals for decades. These companies did offer more exposure but that can no longer be used as excuse after the social media boom. That lump sum usually costs the fighters, artist, or author hundreds of thousands of dollars, and sometimes even several millions of dollars in the long term.

In *Rocky IV*, his protégé pulls up in a nice sports car for Christmas, courtesy of The Duke, of course. Rocky informs his protégé, played by Tommy Morrison, that he would have been able to buy thirty of those sports cars in the future. His protégé is undeterred and drives off in his new sports car.

I say all this to tell you that you can't succeed in what you're trying to do if it's not based on long-term thinking, plain and simple. You can't play the long-term game if you're drowning up to your neck in bills each month. You will need to make the necessary changes in your lifestyle before embarking on your endeavor to see your dreams come true. This might mean you live with a roommate to help with the bills, move into a smaller place, or even the unthinkable, move back home with your parents, if that's even an option.

While I'm quite sure none of these options are ideal, sometimes, to reach success, it requires a small period of time in your life where it's not as comfortable and pleasant as you would like.

Ronnie Coleman had a great catchphrase when he worked out. He would say, “Everybody wants to be a bodybuilder, but don’t nobody want to lift no heavy-ass weight.” This translates to “Everybody wants to be successful, but not everybody is willing to do what’s necessary to reach success.”

Stick to Your Program

There are a lot of pros and cons to being an entrepreneur. Most people probably think it's only pros, but there are some cons as well that I will talk about later. But without a shadow of a doubt one of the biggest positive sides of entrepreneurship is the freedom to make one's own schedule.

When you work a nine-to-five, you work the times and days they give you. With only a few exceptions, they rarely take into account what's convenient for you. You're forced to work hours you don't like or hope they grant you that vacation time you requested three weeks ago.

All this is alleviated once you become your own boss, however. You have the freedom to wake up when you feel like it and work the hours you want to work. Unfortunately, this can be a gift and a curse.

Let me explain. It's easy to work your eight to twelve hours a day when you're an employee because you get fired if you don't. You have your boss to hold you accountable if you don't. When you're your own boss, who do you have to hold you accountable? No one.

And there lies the problem with most entrepreneurs. They simply don't have anyone to hold them accountable, which can mean that it takes a lot of lackadaisical days to get a full day's work done. Here you are at home working on your computer, and it's a beautiful 80 degree day outside. You start to wonder what the beach feels like, or maybe you should call a friend and meet them for lunch. Who is going to stop you, right? You're not going to fire yourself.

If you want to succeed in the game of entrepreneurship, you have to learn how to hold yourself accountable for working the hours you need to work to get your business where you want to get it. I've been my own boss for a few years now, and I can tell you the only way to accomplish this task is by setting a schedule and sticking to it. This means you plan out your day in advance on a calendar, and you don't waver from this schedule for anything, short of a life and death emergency.

I personally use Google Calendar, but any calendar app on your phone should suffice, as long as it has reminders on it. Reminders are when the phone alerts you to your next appointment or task ten to fifteen minutes ahead of time.

The next thing you have to do is have the discipline to not just blow off the reminder whenever you want to do something else. This is where the self-accountability comes into play. There's no calendar app on earth that's going to hold you accountable. That's your responsibility. You just have to remember that you made a schedule for a reason.

Now we're all humans, and I'm well aware of the fact that occasionally you'll forget an important task that might've slipped your mind, but other than these rare occurrences, you should be hell-bent on sticking to the schedule you originally laid out.

With humans, everything can become a habit. Sticking to a schedule is a habit, but unfortunately, not sticking to your schedule can be a habit also. I don't know about you, but I prefer to build habits that are going to cause me more success, not failure.

If you're having trouble sticking to a schedule, you just need to remind yourself of the alternative. It's making your own schedule and sticking to it, or going back into the job force full-time and having a boss give you a schedule you might not like. This principle is two-fold if you're working a full-time or part-time job and building your business on the side.

Here you are, exhausted from working an eight- to twelve-hour shift, and the Lakers game is coming on, but you're getting a reminder from your phone to follow up on some leads you had from the previous week. The fact that you're exhausted from working that nine-to-five should inspire—not deter—you from following up on those leads. Being tired should not be an excuse to become lackadaisical. Use your exhaustion to fuel your motivation to create more income so you can generate passive income.

Pursuing Your Passion Is No Excuse to Quit Your Job or School

Guys ask me all the time on whether they should quit school or their job to pursue their passion. While I'm happy they've discovered what their passion in life is, my answer is always an emphatic *No.*

The fact of the matter is, there is no telling how long it's going to take for your passion to take off. It can literally take years before you're able to make a living pursuing your passion—if ever. Remember pursuing your purpose in life is not about making money; it's about doing what you have a passion for in life. And hopefully, you can figure out a way to make a living at it.

What I advocate for anyone to do is pursue a skill or education first—or simultaneously—while you pursue your purpose. This can usually only be done while you're young and dependent on your parents. If you're older and no longer dependent on your parents, then I suggest working your job and getting an education or skill in your spare time if you haven't discovered your passion in life yet.

On the other hand, if you've discovered your passion in life, then I suggest working your nine-to-five job and working on your purpose in your spare time. The reason I advocate for this is for the simple fact that you need money to pursue your passion. Whether it's to pay bills or raise startup money to get it going, there's always some type of money associated with starting your own business. At the very least, you'll need excess money to hold you over when you decide to make the jump to full-time.

Every entrepreneur has to make the jump at some point. The jump, as I call it, is when an entrepreneur quits his job to become his own boss full-time. No matter how passionate you are about something it's probably the scariest feeling you'll encounter in your lifetime.

If you're a fan of the show *Shark Tank,* you will always notice most entrepreneurs have incurred some type of debt to fund their business. This is not the optimal approach, in my opinion, as you're already hamstringing your potential for growth by already starting out in debt. Instead of using profits to grow the business, they're using their profits to pay debts, hence why they need a shark on the show to invest in the business to help it grow.

Another reason you should not quit your job or not go to school is that you always want to have that foundation to fall back on. I've heard several financial gurus discount having a plan B, as they think it's harboring a defeatist mind-set. I totally disagree with this.

I think if you have a passion in life you should go full force and give it your all, but let's not pretend that sometimes giving something your all sometimes isn't enough. Maybe you have the passion for something but lack the skills necessary to make it a success. We all have our dreams and ambitions, and while I don't want to put doubt into your head about pursuing your passion, I would be negligent if I didn't inform you that building a successful business is still a long shot. Most businesses fail the first year in operation, so having that skill or education is critical to fall back on.

I don't want you to go through life thinking "what if?" How many college athletes have thought they were going to make the pros, only to find out they're not good enough? Well, the chances of having a successful business are about as slim as a college athlete making the pros, if not more. Now, this shouldn't deter you from pursuing your passion in life, as I've already mentioned; this shouldn't be about money anyway. Everyone wants to have their own business. But at the end of the day, we all still have responsibilities, and it's foolish to put all your eggs in one basket and not have a plan B to fall back on.

Prioritizing as an Entrepreneur

When I became a trainer at the gym, I would look at my clients as lifelong clientele. I thought to myself, "Hey, they like me, and I like them. I'm set."

Then they would come to me a few weeks or a couple of months later with some lame excuse as to why they couldn't train anymore. It was sort of went along the lines of "Hey, I'm going to be traveling for work a lot over the oncoming weeks, so maybe we can pick things back up once my schedule settles down?" This would not be a problem, of course, but the only issue was that I would see them back in the gym training by themselves once they returned, without even mentioning to me that they were back in the gym.

I soon realized that their jobs weren't preventing them from training with me; it was them. The lesson I learned is that no matter how much a client likes you or the service you provide, some people just like a variety or to just switch things up.

To be fair, my training abilities weren't as good at the beginning as they would become months later. In business, you have loyal clients and disloyal clients. There's nothing wrong with being a disloyal client. I'm loyal to certain things in my life. I'm loyal to my barber, shopping stores, airlines, etc., mainly due to the fact that I don't see a benefit in changing. Even then, my loyalty is contingent on the service I'm being provided.

On the other hand, I'm not loyal to restaurants, clubs, bars, gyms, etc. because I like a change of scenery. This disloyal bunch is what we refer to as "the 80 percent" in business. This simply means 80 percent of your business will be turnover.

This shouldn't be a problem as long as you're able to replace the existing customers with new customers. You should always be in the process of acquiring new customers. The problem arises when you don't replace the old customers.

If you're good at what you do, you will encounter your share of loyal customers as well. These are the individuals you should build your lifestyle from, and by lifestyle, I'm referring to living expenses. While there are never any guarantees, these individuals will ride with you as long as you're in business, unless a real emergency arises, and they no longer can afford to do business with you, or you have a drop in the quality of service you're offering.

Never take loyal customers for granted and become complacent. Complacency is a business killer. This loyal bunch of individuals will usually make up about 20 percent of your clientele. This is commonly referred to as the 80/20 rule, also known as the Pareto principle.

This principle works in many areas of society, not just with business. Another situation with the 80/20 rule that I've found to be true is that 80 percent of your income will come from that loyal 20 percent of clientele also. This simple fact is just another example of why your loyal clientele should get preferential treatment, as long as it is within reason.

I've canceled or rescheduled on revolving clientele to train my loyal clientele if their schedules called for it. I would do this because I knew deep down these were the individuals I depended on. I wanted my loyal clients to know their loyalty was appreciated by me.

In business, most of your patrons or clientele will be here today, gone tomorrow, but once you get a consistent clientele, you're pretty much set as far as business goes.

The Truth about Entrepreneurship

It might seem from the outside that having your own business is about showing up to work whenever you want to and playing golf all day while your employees work and make you rich, all while you're working fifteen-hour workweeks. I can tell you from my experience as an entrepreneur that this is totally false.

As an entrepreneur, you work more not less. Well, at least initially, while you're building it, you will be. As an entrepreneur, your days never end. You literally can expect to work from sunup to sundown, if you want a successful business. When you're an employee, you work your eight-hour shift, unless you're a teacher or some other profession that requires you to complete your work once you get home.

So as an employee, you actually have more free time than your boss, more than likely, unless it's an established business that has been operating for several years already. If you're an entrepreneur that has employees, it can also get stressful due to the fact that you have other people depending on you to provide an income so that they can provide for their families.

When you're an entrepreneur you're responsible for providing your own insurance and safety net. By "safety net," I mean you more than likely won't qualify for benefits if your business starts to tank. You may qualify for assistance during the startup phase. This is called self-employment assistance. But otherwise you're on your own.

This is fine in my book, as this all-or-nothing mind-set is what most entrepreneurs need to push them to their limits, and you have your skill or education to fall back on in a worst-case scenario. One—if not the best—asset to being your own boss is that your work ethic and determination defines your pay.

This same holds true in most sales jobs. I love an environment where my pay is determined by my work ethic as I will never let anyone outwork me. When you're an employee, your pay rate is determined by your boss. Unless you're in sales, it doesn't really matter how hard you work, your pay is predetermined.

As an employee your hard work can be rewarded with a raise or promotion, but we all know job politics play a big part in that also. Job politics, also commonly known as brownnosing or kissing the boss' behind, is probably the biggest reason I wanted to become my own boss. As a trainer working at one of the gyms in Manhattan, I would commonly see less skilled trainers get lead after lead after lead, while I—who had way more knowledge—would never get any. Never mind the fact that I would never see them even attempt to prospect their own clients.

This is job politics 101. The reason I never got leads is because I never kissed the managers' behinds. I would see other trainers in the office kissing up to the boss for leads. I would just get mine off the floor by myself. I would be lying if I didn't say that this pissed me off from time to time, though. These kinds of job politics are what would eventually push me toward becoming my own boss.

Being Open-Minded to Change

A lot of you are going to read this book and think to yourself, "I can't even visualize myself being something other than a machine operator, factory worker, janitor, etc." because most of us have been programmed to accept nothing but mediocrity, myself included. When I was working the typical nine-to-five job, I never could have dreamed of becoming a bestselling author. I barely liked to read for god's sake. I'm more of an audiobook man myself because of the multitasking capabilities.

I heard a phrase that has stuck with me all these years later. "If you want to hear God laugh, tell him your plan." This saying simply means that only God knows what's in store for you. If someone had told me twelve years ago that by the time I turned forty years of age, I would have already been living in New York for over ten years, I would have thought they were high on drugs. I would have thought to myself, "How is that even possible?" or "I don't even know anyone in New York."

Let's suppose they then said, "You're going to be the most popular dating and life coach on YouTube with a bestselling book." I really would have thought they were crazy. The fact of the matter is, sometimes people come into our lives and change the entire course of our lives. I can remember back home in Alabama around the year 2003. I was very overweight, eating fast food every day and drinking alcohol every night.

One night, going into a nightclub, I would meet a woman that would later change my life. She was a fitness competitor, so her diet was on point. I remember vividly telling her not to try to change me. A few months later, we moved in together. One day on a Saturday, she got up and said, "I'm headed to the gym."

I didn't want to be in the house bored by myself, so I said, "I'm going with you."

After that first workout, I was literally sprung all over again. I had previously got addicted to working out when I was twenty years old but stopped shortly thereafter. If I had never met that fitness competitor, who knows. With my diet being what it was at the time, maybe I would have ended up on *My 600-lb Life*. That woman changed the entire course of my life up to that point. If I had stayed on the course I was going, personal training would have been out of the question.

Let's fast-forward a few more years, and now this is the time that social media is starting to take off—Facebook specifically. I'm just on Facebook doing my normal useless, time-wasting post for the day. All of sudden, I notice a woman who went to the same high school I went to, but I didn't recognize her. But I thought she was pretty, so I sent a friend request. This would lead to an long-distance relationship online that would eventually lead me to coming to New York.

Let's fast forward a few months later, and now I'm in New York looking for a job. My plan was to learn a trade at night while I worked in the daytime. During the initial conversation with one of the gentlemen enrolling me into the program, he notices I'm a fairly large individual. He then proceeds to tell me that he has a cousin who has a security company and that maybe I could make some extra cash on the weekend while I get a trade.

Little did I know that this would eventually lead to me being able to stay in New York, since my relationship with the young lady I met on Facebook would end shortly afterward. Had I not gotten that security job when I did, I simply wouldn't have been able to afford to live in New York, as I already had gone through the little savings that I had come with.

One night, while working security another individual would change the course of my life once again. It was early in the night, so he came over to spark a conversation about my workout regimen, since he noticed I was an abnormally large individual. We talked about thirty minutes, or maybe even a little longer, before he would tell me something that would change the course of my life once again. He said, "Maybe you should pursue fitness, so you don't have to do security" or something to that effect. I remember being furious at first but later using that anger to pursue my passion in fitness. It's safe to say that maybe my life would be totally different had I not met so many individuals who would change the course of my life.

Although you might not know exactly how you're going to get there, you never know when you're going to meet someone who can change the path of your life. The key is to be open to change. Had I been closed-minded about moving to New York, working security, or pursuing fitness for a living, it really wouldn't have mattered that those individuals came into my life. You have to be open to change if you want your life to change.

Laws of Attraction

In life, there aren't any shortcuts to success. You get out what you put into it, plain and simple. If you work hard, get a skill or education, keep your living expenses to a minimum, and save your money to invest, there's a very good chance you'll be successful. On the other hand, if you coast through life and decide to not pursue an education or skill, and live above your means so you don't have anything to invest, there's a very good chance you're going to struggle in life.

In my life experience, I've always noticed that when I had a positive mind-set toward something particular, something positive eventually came from it. If you want to succeed in life, you have to genuinely believe in your heart that if you put in the work, things will work out.

Don't misunderstand what I'm saying, as it's not going to be easy. The law of attraction doesn't mean you won't encounter obstacles in your life, or that doors won't slam in your face. You will still encounter rejections along the way, but this is where the law of attraction comes in handy. If you truly believe in it, then you know it's just a matter of time before you start hearing *Yes*.

People who are ignorant to the law of attraction, or simply don't believe in it, are at a big disadvantage because this is what generally causes them to give up much too quickly. Building your own business will not be an easy task. It takes a lot of perseverance to see your end goal of your dreams coming true. It's really a big advantage to know your hard work will be rewarded in the end.

How to Start a Business

Starting a business is actually easier than you might think. I recommend using Legal Zoom. They'll do most of the groundwork for you, like filing with the state. Afterward, they'll send you a package in the mail that walks you through each step you will need to do to finalize your LLC or business formation, like the publication process.

Of course, you can do it on your own, but in my opinion, it's not worth doing on your own to save a couple hundred bucks, especially if it's your first time. This is why it's so important to have a high-paying skill—or a cash cow, as I like to call it—so it can fund your business startup. The last thing you want to do is be going into debt starting your business. Do it if you have to, but it should be a last resort.

Before you do anything, make sure to have a well-thought-out business plan. I made this mistake when starting my security company. I was just so gung-ho in starting my business that I actually didn't do any research as to what it actually takes to start and build a security business in New York. This simple mistake cost me a lot of money, as I didn't even know the first step of actually getting business. I recommend having a well-thought-out business plan and strategy for building your business before getting started.

Starting a business can be one of the biggest investments you'll make in life, and like all investments you should make sure you've done your homework. Ask yourself questions like, Is this a good business idea for my location? How much of a need is there for this service I'm providing or product in the market place? What's a realistic timetable for when I can expect my business to gain traction? How long will it be before I can expect to start making a profit? Just to name a few questions you should be asking yourself.

Once you've gotten yourself incorporated, you need to make sure you separate your personal finances from business finances. This will protect your personal assets if you're ever sued in the future.

I recommend using different banks also. That's not a requirement, but it does add an extra layer of security in case you're ever sued. Any mingling of the finances could cause you to lose your LLC protection. Any profits from the business should always be put into your business checking or savings account. There are several banks that offer interest rates that exceed inflation.

You should pay yourself a salary from the business profits. Do understand that a lot of entrepreneurs don't pay themselves a salary for quite a while, unless they absolutely have to. They do this to reinvest the money into the business to get it going. The length one can do this depends on living expenses and savings they have acquired. This is why it's so vital to lower your living expenses and have an adequate savings before starting your entrepreneur endeavor.

Maybe you haven't noticed a common theme here, but planning well ahead should be something you seriously consider before starting a business.

How to Get Business

Starting a business is pretty simple for the most part, but getting business is the key to whether you'll succeed or not. When you're starting a business and offering your services or product to the marketplace, you should ask yourself, Why should potential customers try my service or product? Your product or service should be unique in its own way.

I'm not saying it has to reinvent the wheel, but what I am saying is that it has to stand out from other competitors' products. Humans are creatures of habit and hate change for the most part. You have to incentivize potential customers to try your product or service.

When I started following fitness channels on YouTube, by no means were The Hodgetwins, C.T. Fletcher, or Kali Muscle, the most knowledgeable channels on YouTube. But they were by far the most entertaining, which, in turn, incentivized me to watch their channels over the more knowledgeable channels, since I would gain fitness knowledge while simultaneously being entertained. Judging by the number of subscribers on these channels, I wasn't the only one who felt this way.

Unfortunately, just being unique won't do it. See, it was easy for me to watch The Hodgetwins, C. T. Fletcher, and Kali Muscle because it cost me nothing, so I had nothing to lose. When you're offering your service or product to the marketplace, you're expecting customers to shell out their cold, hard cash. Customers have a tendency to stick to what they know works.

Usually, to get these individuals' business, some sort of deal has to be given. There's a reason lawyers and CPAs offer a free one-hour consultation. There's a reason some mechanical shops offer a free diagnostic test. There's a reason why businesses offer sales, other than to clear inventory. This is usually done to get potential customers to sample their product or service.

While no one really enjoys giving their products or service away for free, it's practically essential to gain traction in business. What giving away your product or service for free does is it takes the risk away from potential customers, which in turns gives them a sense of "Hey, what do I have to lose?" It also sends a clear message that you believe in your product or service so much that you're willing to give it away for free, because you know once they try it, they'll be willing to come back.

This is the same assurance that customers are given with a money back guarantee. When you watch an infomercial, and they announce they're offering a ninety-day money-back guarantee, the first thing that goes through your mind is "I have nothing to lose. If it doesn't work, I'll send it back." Also, if nobody knows who you are, you have to show them or sell them on your level of expertise.

When that lawyer or CPA gives you that free one-hour consultation, what they're trying to do is show you their level of expertise and how they can benefit you. My first book was a bestseller, and hopefully, this one will be also. But if I hadn't put dozens of free videos on YouTube to display my level of expertise in dating, I doubt that would have happened. By giving away so much information for free to prove myself, it allowed me to have a customer base to sell to.

Bring Value to the Marketplace

In life, you always have your haves and have-nots. It has been that way since the beginning of time. The have-nots are usually jealous of how easy the haves seem to make their money compared to themselves.

The have-nots usually have a job in which they trade time for money. Other than a few occupations, this is rarely a recipe for financial success. On the other hand, the haves usually make a lot more money with less work, or at least it seems that way.

There's a phrase, "The harder you work the less you make." This phrase should be "the harder you work manually, the less you work." I don't work hard manually, as in physically, but mentally, I work very hard. When I did manual labor, I worked hard physically but very little mentally. Now it's the complete opposite.

Fortunately for me, you make more money when you work hard mentally as opposed to physically. That's because when you work hard mentally, it usually revolves around some form of creativity. Creativity is one of the building blocks for wealth creation. It simply boils down to what you bring to the marketplace.

If you want to make money, you have to generate money. NFL or NBA players make millions because they generate millions. When you watch an NFL game on television, the network has paid the NFL billions to broadcast those games on their network, not to mention all the money generated from stadium ticket sales, concession stands, merchandise sales, licensing, etc. The networks can pay this sum of money due to the amount of money advertisers will to pay for a few seconds of advertising. The advertisers are willing to pay such a large sum due to the ratings the NFL generates. This is capitalism at its finest.

Musicians are paid really well, depending on the contract, of course. Whenever their album or song is played on the radio, they receive a small royalty, but it adds up when they have thousands of radio stations around the world playing their music. The same formula is at play here. The radio stations can afford to pay this royalty due to the number of advertisers willing to pay for ad time.

If you make minimum wage, it simply means you bring very little value to the marketplace. You have to find a way to serve, help, or entertain more people at once. By serve, I simply mean that you have some type of product or service to offer to the marketplace.

While being financially successful is never easy, financial success is not about how hard you work, but rather, how much value you bring to the marketplace.

Why You Can't Stay Focused

One common obstacle that most individuals come across as they embark on their journey to entrepreneurship is actually staying focused on their goal. The reason this is a problem is because when you start pursuing your passion, it usually pays nothing at the beginning. In fact, in most situations, it's actually probably costing you money, or at the very least, a lot of your spare time with no financial reward.

To rid yourself of this lack of focus, you have to develop the long-term mind-set. The hardest thing to develop on your path of entrepreneurship is the long-term mind-set and delayed gratification. Most individuals, myself included, have been programmed all our lives to trade time for money. So when we work and don't receive some type of immediate financial benefit, our first natural impulse is to think "Something is not right. If I work, aren't I supposed to be paid?"

This is a subconscious thought that gets many would-be entrepreneurs sidetracked. These thoughts will continue to permeate throughout your conquest unless you adopt a long-term thinking mind-set.

Another thing that helped me stay on course, unlike other times in my life when I would start something only to lose motivation, was that I simply had reached a point where I was sick and tired of being sick and tired.

When I was a bouncer working at a high-end nightclub in Manhattan, I would often watch the club patrons enjoy bottles of wine and champagne worth hundreds of dollars. I would also think to myself, why are they able to enjoy such a wonderful luxurious lifestyle, while I work for $30,000 a year in New York? I'm smart; why can't I do the same? This thought would enter my mind basically every night for the next three years while I worked this club. As I've mentioned earlier, a talk with a club patron would change the course of my life forever, but that talk wouldn't have meant anything if I hadn't reached a point in my life where I was sick and tired of being sick and tired.

There were multiple times in my life where I would start something without seeing it through. I went to Job Corps when I was nineteen years old, only to get homesick a month later and go home. I enrolled in college in my early twenties, only to quit the first semester. I even tried enrolling into the armed forces, only to back out at the last moment.

See, at that point in my life I wasn't fed up with my living situation. Everyone reaches this breaking point at different ages in their life. Unfortunately for me, it didn't hit me until I was well into my thirties. Some individuals reach it at a very early age, while others don't reach it until much later in life, if at all. I have older family members who are content with living a mediocre lifestyle. I'm not here to tell anyone how they should live their life, but for me mediocrity was no longer a choice.

Business Partners

Once you decide to pursue your passion for a living, you might have the idea of taking on business partners, or even worse, friends as business partners. Unless it's someone that was there at the origin of thought, or they provide a necessary skill set that you yourself simply don't have, I see no need for business partners. If you're a driven person, you must understand that most individuals won't be as driven as you are.

This means instead of you spending your energy being productive, you'll spend it trying to motivate someone to spend more time working. It also can put you in a dependency mind-set. When you're pursuing your passion solo you know it's up to you to get everything done. When you have partners, you have a tendency to start depending on others to complete the task at hand instead of you just doing what needs to be done.

In the future, if you decide to take your business in a different direction, you won't have to confer with a business partner. In business, things don't always go according to plan. Sometimes you're forced to adapt on the fly. Your vision might change while your business partner's might stay the same or vice versa. You want to spend your energy growing your business, not trying to sell your business partner on which direction you should take the business. It's hard enough to sell to customers without having to try and sell to your business partner every time you have an idea.

Divorcing a business partner is almost as bad as divorcing a spouse. Unless you can come to a peaceful agreement, the courts have to get involved. This, of course, means getting lawyers involved which means you're spending resources on legal fees instead of directing those same resources to grow the business. This could set your business back financially for many months and, in some cases, many years. If it's a friend, it could end the friendship altogether.

In my opinion, it's not worth taking on a business partner unless it's a necessary skill set that they bring to the table, and even then, I would try to see if there's a way if I could learn that skill set myself. Once you've learned how to properly invest your money, the only business partners you'll ever need is your money. I look at money as a tool to make me more money, not as a tool to buy *stuff*. Therefore, technically I'm in business with my money.

Branding

One of the biggest aspects to starting your business that's overlooked is branding. Branding is how potential clients and customers can identify you. Branding shows that you're a legit business.

You should never invest too much money in the beginning, but branding, for the most part, does not require a ton of money to get done. You can find many artists on Google or business apps like Thumbtack, where logo designers compete for your business.

You should try to find a name for your business which is unique and different but represents your brand. Take my brand for example, Alpha Male Strategies. That name embodies everything I'm doing as a dating and life coach. I'm teaching primarily beta males everything you need to be an alpha male, which, coincidentally, is more than just casually sleeping with a ton of women. To be a *complete* alpha male, you must be your own man, a.k.a. your own boss.

Don't get me wrong; it's not beta to work for someone else, but a true alpha male would never be content with working for someone all his life. A true, all-around alpha male would work for someone else while simultaneously building something of their own on the side.

After you've figured out your business name you should pick a logo that represents your brand. Remember, your name and logo are usually what potential clients and customers see first. It's where a lot of subconscious decisions are made as to whether or not an individual wants to do business with you.

It's sort of like what a book cover and title do for you when you're browsing books to read. If the book has a catchy cover, title, or a combination of the both, you're more inclined to buy it. Some books are crappy, but the packaging was good, so you bought it. But on the other hand, some of the best books ever written were looked over initially due to poor packaging.

The same can be said for thumbnails or video titles on YouTube. If your thumbnail or title isn't catchy enough, you won't get as many views as you would if you had used a catchy thumbnail or title. Humans are visual creatures, and if something catches our attention, you have a good chance to get our business, or at the very least, we'll check your product out.

In business, all you can ask for is someone to try your product. After you've gotten them to sample what you're offering, it's just a matter of whether they like your product at that point. If they don't like your product, it doesn't necessarily mean your product isn't good. We all have different tastes and interests. Someone not liking your product could simply mean your product isn't for them. It's nothing personal.

Usually over time, if enough people sample and like your product, the word gets out, and your product starts to sell, but sometimes this could be many months or, in some cases, years later.

The take-home message here is that packaging matters a great deal when trying to build your business, so make sure you put a lot of time and effort into how you want your product presented.

Let the Business Build Itself

A lot of entrepreneurs make the mistake of spending a ton of money up front before the business is making money. I made this mistake initially, only to find out it's totally unnecessary for the most part. I'm not going to kid you and pretend like you don't have to spend some money to get your business going, but it should be kept minimal as possible.

The reason you want to do this is because you want to spend the money where it's needed, and most times, this is not where you would have thought initially. When I started my security business, I spent a lot of money on Google ads thinking that was where I would get business. I did get available security guards applying for jobs but very little business.

I then had logos printed up on T-shirts along with my website. This might not be an issue if you're flush with cash, but if you're financially strapped, as most entrepreneurs are in the beginning, you'll quickly regret this decision.

You should let the business build itself. This means as you start to make money, you want to put as much of it as you can back into the business. All of it would be ideal, if possible. I recommend it being done this way because you want to save those resources to ensure you're able to pursue your passion in the long term because it's probably not going to be an overnight thing. This means if you squander all your resources on unnecessary expenses at the beginning, you're more likely to end up having to spend some of your valuable time to make ends meet, so to speak, later on.

To build your business, your greatest asset is your time, not money, so if you're spending time to make ends meet, that's time that you're not spending to build your business. To build your business, it's going to take a great commitment of your time. This is why, in the beginning, you want to be very diligent in how you spend it. The longer you can go without having to acquire more income elsewhere the more time you can invest into your business, therefore giving you a much better opportunity to build your business.

Vices

Life, in itself, is not easy. For most, life revolves around working a job you hate, paying bills, paying taxes, raising children, and death. Life can be downright boring at times, and people, since the beginning of time, have always tried to find a way to entertain themselves.

This can be quite depressing to some, so most people develop some sort of vice to escape mentally from the daily grind of life. These vices can include drinking, drugs, shopping, gambling, clubbing, eating, and chasing women among others. Some people go the relationship route, even if the person isn't exactly what they want, due to the fact they have the mind-set that someone is better than nothing.

You can only imagine how unsatisfying these relationships are. These individuals never can last long in a relationship because they always come across extremely needy. A needy person is someone who relies on someone else to keep them company in some type of way. That could be through texting, calling, or in person. It really doesn't matter, as long as you're giving them attention. Unless they're lucky enough to meet an individual as needy as them, they'll never be able to keep a mate long term.

Nobody should be your life; they should only add to your life. The average individual works eight hours a day and sleeps about six to eight hours a day. This leaves approximately eight to ten hours of the day that an individual needs to fill with some type of activity.

You have two types of ways you can fill this time. It can be filled productively or unproductively. Watching TV is a horrible, unproductive way to fill this time, as it does nothing to enhance your life. Sure, we all have our favorite shows we like, but if you're the individual who, once he or she gets off work and flops in front of the TV for hours, you'll never accomplish anything.

There's a reason entertainers and athletes are paid millions and millions of dollars. People want to be entertained and are willing to spend a lot of money for it. As bad as watching TV is, it pales in comparison to how unproductive it is to engage in vices that waste time and money. At least watching television isn't draining your bank account. Vices can create expensive habits that can destroy households in some cases. Simply put, acquiring a vice is just adding another liability.

Once you've engaged in a vice, it usually requires some type of counseling to overcome it. There's only one way to overcome this void you're trying to fill, and that's to find your purpose in life. Pursuing your passion in life not only makes you more attractive, due to the fact you won't come across needy, but it also gives you life. Not to mention, you'll spend your free time doing what you love instead of engaging in vices that are draining your bank account.

It's been said that once you've developed a bad habit the only thing that can break it is another vice. I suggest letting that vice be pursuing your purpose in life. Pursuing your purpose kills that need for mindless bank-draining entertainment.

My life always felt like it was missing something until I found my purpose in life. I used to club five nights a week and chase women to fill my free time. This was obviously very expensive and time-consuming. If I had invested that money into assets instead of clubbing and chasing women, who knows how much money I would have accumulated by now.

Business Names and Logos

Some entrepreneurs make the mistake of trying to get their business name and logo trademarked during the business startup phase. From my experience, this is could be a mistake.

First off, you get some protection from the state once you publicly use your name. Secondly, getting your business officially federally trademarked can be more expensive than you think, unless you're able to get it upon first submission, which is extremely rare.

If the US Patent and Trademark Office (USPTO) rejects your initial application, they'll send you what is called an office action. This office action is usually sent because your trademark application wasn't detailed or specific enough. In other words, it's too vague. Once you receive your office action from the USPTO, you'll need to hire a professional trademark lawyer to submit your trademark application with more detail than before. This resubmission isn't free, by the way, and neither is the trademark lawyer you'll need to hire this time around to have a chance to get it through. Oh yes, there's still a chance the USPTO could still reject your resubmission of the application. No lawyer would ever make the mistake of guaranteeing you anything.

You, of course, could make the foolish mistake of trying to resubmit the application yourself, which I wouldn't advise, by the way, but it's your money. If you want to give it a try, knock yourself out. As you can see, this can become very costly very quickly.

Making a mistake of this magnitude in the beginning stages could really hamper your financial longevity in how long you can afford to spend so much time building something in your free time. This, by the way, is a liability in the startup phase. Hopefully, you can build it until it becomes an asset, but most startups are a liability initially, until they start making income.

There's no need to spend valuable resources on obtaining federally registered trademarks until your business is making money, unless money isn't an issue for you whatsoever. But even then, you have no idea how long you'll need to build your business.

Savings

You shouldn't even think about building a business full-time unless you have an adequate savings of at least a year's worth of living expenses. The key thing there is if you're planning on pursuing your passion full-time. You don't need a year's worth of savings if you're pursuing your passion part-time.

Ideally, one shouldn't try to build a business full-time unless it's starting to turn some type of profit. Don't quit your job to build something that isn't turning a profit yet. You should do both at the same time until your business is profitable.

I know most individuals hate their job and can't wait to quit, but this is very irresponsible in my opinion. Businesses can take a very long time to build in most cases. If you really want to focus on building your business full-time, you will need an adequate savings.

To obtain this savings, it will require one or two things. You'll either need to sacrifice for a while leading up to the time you would want to pursue your passion full-time. This means limiting your living expenses for the time being. These limitations can range anywhere from dating, dining with friends, clothing, and even cable, if need be. It'll be bologna sandwiches for you for the time being.

The other option is to make more money, which would require working some overtime if it's available, or even obtaining a second job. Building a business aside, every working adult should strive to have at least three months' worth of savings available, in case life takes you on one of the roller-coaster rides that life takes you on. Preferably, six months' worth of savings would be ideal.

There are three things in life that are guaranteed: death, taxes, and life's uncertainties. That uncertainty can be anything from losing your job to getting ill. Having savings can be the difference between losing your job being a minor inconvenience or losing everything and having to move in with friends or family temporary. I would even recommend additional savings if you work a volatile job like social media or sales. Social media platforms have the right to take down pages at will if they don't like the content the creator is posting, or if they deem it as hate speech.

If you work a highly volatile job, you should strive to have at least a year's worth of living expenses saved up. After you've saved this much, you really should think about investing and letting your money work for you. I really see no benefit in having more than that saved up, unless you're saving to invest in something down the road later, like real estate or a business venture. The stock market is always a good place to start. Just make sure you do your homework on whatever you decide to invest in.

I recommend putting your savings into an online banking account. They give the best interest rates due to the fact they have very little overhead, since most of them don't have any physical branches. They usually offer at least a 2 percent interest rate on your savings. These banks include American Express, Ally Bank, Discover Card, and others.

Physical branches typically offer less than a 1 percent interest rate. The 2 percent interest rate at least keeps up with inflation. If you're going to have your money in a savings account you might as well try to get as much interest as you possibly can, unless you enjoy losing money, because that's what happens if you put your money into a savings account that doesn't keep up with inflation.

Health Insurance

Health insurance is something every individual needs, and thanks to the Affordable Care Act, it's something every individual can obtain, due to having no restrictions on preexisting conditions.

Now, I know some people might think that it's expensive, but that doesn't mean it's not affordable. Unfortunately, we live in a society where people would rather spend money on a couple of international trips than pay for their healthcare. In my nearly forty years on this earth, there's one thing I've always noticed about most people I've encountered in my lifetime: their priorities are not in the correct order.

What you pay in health insurance is based on what you make. An individual who makes well into the six-figure range can expect to pay more than someone who makes just above the poverty line. The reason this is an issue is because most individuals live neck and neck with their income, so when you compound that with a higher premium, they start to pout, when in actuality they should factor in their health insurance just as though they would their car insurance. Then this would not be an issue.

It always amazes me that people have no issue insuring their car to drive but cry when they have to pay high premiums for health insurance. People care more about driving a luxury vehicle than they do about their health. The reason most people cry about health insurance is because most people have the absurd notion that they'll never get sick. This just so happens to be the primary reason individuals do not save money for a rainy day. People never anticipate the inevitable trials and tribulations that arise throughout one's lifetime.

Hopefully, you're one of the lucky ones who never loses their job or gets sick, but people get sick or lose their job every day. Going without insurance is not only playing Russian roulette with your life, but it is also gambling with your finances. Hospital bills cause a lot of financial crises in America every day. You'll sleep so much better at night knowing you're covered if you get sick. I know we live in a world where everyone would rather spend that money on shopping or driving a better car, but if you truly want financial and mental peace you are going to have to learn how to prioritize your life. Health insurance should not be considered a luxury but a necessity in my book.

Social Circle

You are what you hang around. There's very little doubt that we are products of our environment. You have to surround yourself with individuals who are positive and have the same goals as you. You can't expect to hang out with individuals who have negative, unambitious energy without expecting that to hurt your chances of accomplishing your goals.

There's a theory that the five individuals you spend the most time with have the greatest influence on you. From my experience in life, I've found this to be pretty accurate. Birds of a feather flock together.

If your goal is to be a successful entrepreneur, you need to have friends that also have this goal in mind, or at the very least, encourage you to push through if you start doubting yourself. These individuals tell you things like "Hey, push through it" or "Give it time."

On the other hand, if you hang around the wrong crowd, they'll just say things that reinforce self-doubt like "I told you it wasn't going to work" or "It's going to take you forever to build that business." They tell you these things because deep down, they don't want you to be successful.

You have to understand misery loves company. They want you working a crappy nine-to-five like them so you can all be miserable together. See, you must understand, if you have uninspired friends, your success is like holding up a mirror to them and exposing their shortcomings.

This doesn't mean you should go out and cut off all your friends because they don't share your entrepreneurial spirit, but once you see any negative behavior from them coming in your direction you should limit this relationship as soon as possible. It's hard enough as it is to stay motivated when business isn't great. The last thing you need in your life is someone bringing more doubt into your life.

How to Give a Great Interview

Now that you have your newly acquired skill or education, it's time to get a return on your investment by obtaining employment. Life is a process, so before you launch the next *Fortune* 500 company, I recommend getting a job.

This job will finance your business idea or the investments you're considering. That business idea isn't going to finance itself, and those assets aren't going to buy themselves. You can't skip steps when trying to obtain wealth.

Lazy people will point to some fortunate billionaires like Bill Gates and Mark Zuckerberg who dropped out of college as examples of why learning a skill or obtaining an education aren't needed to obtain wealth. I would counter that claim by suggesting guys like that are outliers and not the norm. Lazy people, looking to cut corners, always find outliers to excuse their lazy behavior.

As a dating and life coach, I tell guys to become the best version of themselves to increase their dating options. There isn't a day that goes by that I'm not told of how some fat, broke guy they know has women. They use that outlying example as an excuse to not put in the work.

Before you go get all gung-ho about becoming the next Warren Buffett, you first have to get the job that's going to be the launching pad or cash cow for all of this. The first step in creating wealth, is to get income coming in to invest.

This means you're going to have to go on interviews. Skilled jobs or occupations that require a level of education usually require an interview process. In some cases, this might require interviewing more than once. It really just boils down to how sought-out of a job it is. Usually the more qualified applicants are, the more stringent the interviewing process.

This is actually a good sign. A job that hires people right off the street usually isn't a job worth wanting. Those type of jobs offer very little by the way of benefits, and the pay usually isn't all that great, hence the lack of job applicants.

The most important aspect to remember when going through an interviewing process is to remember you're trying to make a great first impression. You only have one opportunity to make a great first impression. With that being said, you should be on time to the interview, and by on time, I mean about fifteen to twenty minutes early. This is to ensure you're on time even if there's a minor traffic slowdown. If you're commuting during peak hours, I would even go as far as to say that thirty minutes early wouldn't be a bad idea.

You should be dressed nicely. This doesn't mean you have to wear a tuxedo but pretty damn close. I recommend a button up dress shirt, tucked in, with a blazer on top if the weather permits. You can wear jeans or slacks, but make sure your pants are all the way around your waist with a belt. There should be absolutely no sagging whatsoever.

You should be well groomed. This means if you have cornrows or dreadlocks, they should be freshly done. If you have facial hair, this should be trimmed neatly.

If you aren't taking the interviewing process serious, then why should the employer take you seriously? If he's doing interviews, then it's a high probability that he has multiple applicants. Something as simple as looking neat can be the deciding factor on a good paying job.

You should sound like you're excited even being considered for the position. Employers are looking for passion, because they know these are the individuals that are more than likely to bring some value to the company. Employers don't like to hire individuals who they think are just looking for a job to pass time until something better comes along. Employers prefer hiring individuals they think will last twenty years not twenty days.

Ask questions about the company. Try to sound like you really want to be there. Reaffirm why you think you're the best option for the job. This could be talking about your passion for the job and skills or education you've obtained leading up to the job. You're basically selling yourself to the interviewer, and by selling yourself, I mean you're selling the value you could bring to the employer.

What Type of Job to Pursue

The type of job to pursue is very important. I recommend choosing a job that will prepare you to be your own boss one day if you have found your purpose in life.

This means that if you have a passion for fitness, then you should consider working for a gym. Working for this gym would not only allow you build your clientele base, but it would more than likely enhance your abilities as a trainer as well as your marketing skills.

When you're an independent trainer you can run into the mentality of thinking you know it all. I was in for a rude awakening when I started working for a gym. I quickly discovered that I wasn't nearly as knowledgeable as I thought I was. Working for this gym not only taught me valuable skills that I would later use to retain pretty much all of my clients until I stopped training, but it also taught me valuable marketing skills I would use to obtain more clients.

The gym was notorious for giving clients a free session. This free session is valuable in obtaining new clients. It allows the clients to observe your training style, so they know if it will be a good fit. If you have a passion for fitness, I have no idea how being a mechanic is going to enhance your abilities as a trainer. Secondly, even if the mechanic job paid you more money, you would spend the days counting the hours down. If you're going to spend one third of your workdays working, why not do something you actually enjoy and can help get you one step closer to financial freedom?

If you haven't discovered what you have a passion for, then I would recommend going into a field that is in high demand. People complain that they have a worthless degree but still have to pay Sallie Mae every month. This is because they chose a field that's not in high demand. For example, science, technology, engineering, and mathematics (STEM) fields are high-paying jobs that are high in demand. These fields may be a little more difficult to obtain a degree than your degree in bass fishing, but they are worth it.

You should not just stroll through life not trying to accomplish anything, waiting to discover your purpose in life. The fact of the matter is, you never know how long it may be before you figure out what's your purpose in life. I was thirty-four years old before I pursued my passion, even though I had discovered it many years earlier. It may take you even longer.

Life waits on no man and while it would be ideal for everyone to discover their purpose in life at a very early age, this is not always the case. Let your purpose in life find you. Until then, pursue a field that is in high demand. A skilled trade is also a good route to take. Electricians, plumbers, air conditioning, and refrigeration are all examples of trades that are always in demand.

What to Do in Your Spare Time until You Find Your Purpose

I want to make something clear so you guys don't misunderstand what I'm saying. I don't want you wandering the earth in your spare time, trying to figure out your purpose in life. I wholeheartedly believe your purpose should find you and not the other way around. When I say finding you, I'm simply referring to living a social life of abundance and letting your passion find you.

I'm a big proponent in the law of attraction, and when you engage in activities you genuinely enjoy, I believe things have a way of finding you. Two things you tend to find are love and your purpose in life. We all know you never find anything when you're actively looking for it. Love is like this also. You can only find it when you're not looking for it.

You should only live a social life of abundance, however, if you're making a decent living with what you're doing. I recommend trying to enhance your skill or, perhaps, getting a skill in your spare time if you currently do not have one. It's called sacrificing for a reason, meaning you'll have to sacrifice something to accomplish your goal.

You can't win at chess without sacrificing a few pawns along the way, and you won't become successful without giving up some aspects of your social life. There's always a price to be paid to win in life. How are you going to live a social life of abundance if you're barely making ends meet? Socializing doesn't have to be expensive, but it does cost more than sitting in the house. The gas alone can add up to be a pretty nice sum.

So if you're a plumber, try to see what steps you need to take next to become a master plumber. If you're a welder, maybe you can consider trying to become a master welder. Some plumbers and welders make a decent living as is without becoming certified masters in their respective fields, and if this is the case, then maybe you can afford to live a social life of abundance.

However, if this is not the case, and you're barely making ends meet, then I highly suggest you trying to enhance your skills to increase your income. As a personal trainer, I was always trying to enhance my skills. I was always taking different classes to learn different techniques so I could constantly evolve my clients' programs. In doing so I was able to keep my clients engaged longer thus allowing me to make more money. Those classes weren't free, so this meant I made investments into my business, which just so happened to be my knowledge when it came to being a personal trainer.

A good barometer to test if you can afford to have more of a social life is if you are able to save at least 15 percent of your income at the end of the month. If you aren't, then you should probably try to increase your skills or knowledge to create more income. You can always learn more to increase your income, but I do believe there's such a thing in life as being content.

Not everyone aspires to become wealthy, and I can respect that, as long as you're in a financial situation where you can save at least 15 percent of your monthly income. My reasoning for this is simply that things in life are bound to happen. Health issues, car accidents, layoffs, etc. Something is bound to pop up eventually, and if you're living that close to the edge, you're one slip and fall away from catastrophe.

You want to make sure you have a solid foundation in life. By solid foundation, I'm referring to no debt and three to six months' worth of living expenses in case something catastrophic arises.

I'm all up for anyone who wants to pursue their passion in life, but I'm of the mind-set that it should be done in a responsible way that isn't leaving you open to going into debt or losing everything.

How to Pay Off Debt

There are a lot of factors that come into play when paying off debt. One factor that is often overlooked is the emotional aspect to paying off debt. There are two primary ways to pay off debt. There's paying off the highest interest debt first or paying off the smallest debts first. Paying off the highest interest first makes more sense in practical terms because you save money on interest in the long term.

For instance, you have a credit card company that's charging you a 22 percent interest rate on your card balance, but you have a balance of over $10,000. Depending on how long it takes you to get rid of that outstanding balance, you're going to pay a pretty good bit of money on interest.

The alternative is to pay off a smaller debt even if the interest rate is lower. For instance, you owe $2,000 on a furniture debt, and you've been making the minimum payments on it with an interest rate of 12 percent. The suggestion to eliminate debt this way is based primarily on the factor of accomplishing a mental victory—an emotional victory, if you will.

There are some people who can stick to a clean diet with all kinds of snacks on top of the refrigerator, and there are those who need to rid their house of all sweets and snacks to stick to a diet. There are some individuals who can eat clean 24–7 with very minimal cheating, while on the other hand, there are individuals who have to have a cheat meal at least once or twice a week to stick to a diet.

I said all that to say we're all different. Some people will be able to do the practical approach, which is paying the highest interest rate first, without needing the mental victories of eliminating the smallest debts first. See, when you do the smaller debts first, you get an emotional victory of decreasing the number of creditors you have.

If you're an individual who doesn't feel you'll be able to stick to the program if you don't have a sense of accomplishment by eliminating the smaller debts first, then I suggest you stick to paying off the smaller debts first even if they have a lower interest rate. At the end of the day we're not robots, and the emotional aspect to paying off debt does play a factor.

Life Is about Decisions

In my lifetime, I've had many ups and downs along the way, but when I look back at it all, one thing is abundantly clear to me: life is primarily about decisions. The decisions you make in life will pretty much dictate the course your life will take.

There are a lot of good-hearted men and women in prisons and jails across the world who let one bad decision land them behind bars. When you turn sixteen years of age in the state where I'm originally from, you can legally drop out of school. That's a decision you can make, but please understand that's a decision that can—and in all likelihood, will—haunt you for the rest of your life.

If you've ever had the misfortune of working at a factory, you would know what the daily life of uneducated and unskilled workers looks like. You're way more likely to end up working a job that'll have you living from check to check. Check to check means no savings and definitely no money to invest. To be fair, there are individuals who make good money but still live check to check, thanks to trying to keep up with the Joneses, but I think you get what I'm saying.

No offense, but these will also be the same individuals who count on the government to create higher paying non-skilled jobs to bail them out from their bad decisions. Never depend on the government—or anything else for that matter—to rescue you. You have to rescue yourself.

We all get pissed off from time to time. That doesn't mean you need to let some asshole get you so upset that you punch him in the mouth and land yourself in jail—or even worse, with a prison sentence, if you cause some serious harm. One minute you're eating dinner with your girl, sipping wine, and thirty minutes later you're in the back of a police squad car because you made a bad decision. There's nothing wrong with defending yourself, but other than that you should walk away.

If someone is heckling or taunting you because they're a butthole—and let's face it, there are some jerks in the world—but you just have to learn how to stand your ground without resorting to a physical altercation, unless it's in self-defense. If he's taunting you in a joking way, you should just ignore it altogether and leave the vicinity.

Throughout your lifetime you're going to encounter several situations where a bad decision can have lasting effects. Whether it be going into debt to buy that flat screen TV, purchasing a car that you can barely afford the car loan on, or punching some jerk in the face for taunting you, at the end of the day, it all boils down to making the right decisions in life.

Mental Strength and Toughness

Life gets difficult at times, and therefore, developing some mental toughness is required at times to persevere. Mental toughness does not just develop from the thin air. It comes from being battle-tested and surviving those tough times. Surviving those experiences gives us the confidence that we can survive anything. I guess you can call mental toughness another form of confidence.

Having mental toughness is good, but the main thing about having mental toughness is having the ability to learn from the situation that required you to have mental toughness. Life is really just one big learning experience. This is why wisdom is something that's obtained throughout many of life's lessons.

The need to obtain this mental toughness usually means you were in a predicament that's not too favorable. This unfavorable situation, as unpleasant as it may have been, does have a positive effect. It provided a valuable learning experience.

I can remember when I was young, watching Michael Jordan lead Chicago Bulls in getting bounced from the playoffs every year in the late 80s by the Detroit Pistons. It took a lot of mental toughness to come back year after year and try again and again, only to lose. Each year the Bulls would get closer and closer to dethroning the Pistons until finally dethroning the Pistons in the early 90s. The reason they were able to dethrone them was because each year they would improve on their mistakes and get better and better. They were learning from their mistakes. Learning from their mistakes is what gave them the mental confidence which is the foundation of mental toughness.

Mental toughness serves two functions. It keeps you from wallowing in self-pity in times of despair, and it offers a very valuable learning experience to prevent this type of mistake from happening again in the future.

Significant Others

Without a shadow of a doubt, the person who is going to be the biggest contributor or distraction to you obtaining what you're trying to accomplish, other than yourself of course, will be your significant other. Your significant other can be your spouse, girlfriend, boyfriend, or even someone who you are seriously dating.

The reason they play such a big role in your life is because they can either offer encouragement, or they can offer constant criticisms. These criticisms can come in the lack of communication between you and them, since you spend most of your time focusing on your passion in life. And let's be honest here—most individuals can start to get a little jealous that you're more passionate about something other than them.

Another thing to consider is that your significant other can start to feel a certain type of way by making yourself of higher value. If your significant other is insecure, they won't like the fact that you're becoming of higher value or status. They know that you bettering yourself opens you up to potentially meeting someone else.

You see this a lot when someone in a relationship decides to lose weight. Sometimes, the person they are dating tries to halt their progress. If you see these characteristics in someone you're dating, I would advise you cutting them off immediately. They will only slow your progress, if not kill it altogether. Insecurities in your significant other are only them telling themselves that you can do better.

Whenever I've accomplished any major feats in my life, it was when I was single. I'm not saying that you have to be single to accomplish great things, because there are plenty of successful men who'll be the first one to point out their wife as the biggest driving force behind their success. I wholeheartedly believe that if you can find a supportive significant other to encourage you, then by all means, you should keep them, but I think those are the outliers and not the norm. The average significant other is going to be selfish and demand more of your time.

I can't tell you how many women I've had who complained on my lack of phone communication. If you're trying to build something, you're not going to have all that available time to text back and forth. In situations like this, when your time is very limited you want to hear encouragement not discouragement. How can you put your all into what you're trying to accomplish if you have a disgruntled spouse complaining constantly about you loving your work more than you love them?

For the most part, anything in your life that's not an asset is a liability. This doesn't just hold true in the financial world, but it holds true in your social life as well. If you have friends, family, or a spouse that are not adding to your life, then it'll probably serve you better to sever those relationships, or at the very minimum, cut down socializing with them.

Red Flags You Should Not Be Friends with Someone

Significant others in our lives are not the only individuals that can hamper your success. If you make friends with the wrong individuals, they, too, can slow your grind but also cause a lot of turmoil in your life, if they're the jealous type.

There's a saying that we're the sum of the five people we spend the most time with. Who you decide to hang with has a great influence on which path you take in life. If you're hanging with a bunch of lazy, unambitious individuals who only want to smoke weed in their free time, how long is it before this kind of behavior starts to impact your way of thinking? On the other hand, if you're hanging with individuals who are goal-orientated, positive-minded, and hardworking, this type of behavior will most likely have a positive influence on you.

If nothing else, you'll want to step your game up to remain friends with them. Subconsciously, you have to figure that they only want to associate with like-minded people. Birds of a feather flock together. With all this being said, there are some signs that you can spot if someone isn't a genuine friend. The reason that picking the proper friends is even in this book is because we're not robots. We have emotions, and when you associate yourself with the wrong people, they can wear on your emotions. Instead of focusing on your goals, you find yourself pissed off at something they did or said.

A genuine friend initiates contact, just like a woman who is genuinely interested in you or a friend who calls to check on you from time to time. If you find yourself having to initiate contact every time, there's a good chance that if you stop initiating contact, you would probably never hear from them again. It stands to reason that they're merely tolerating you at this point. You have to value yourself as a person with qualities that other people would love to associate themselves with.

True friends invite their friends to their get-togethers and gatherings. If you have to find out about a friend's party via social media or hearsay, it stands to reason that they don't want you there. If it's a true friend, you don't get invited at the last minute. They tell you way in advance, just to make sure you have made arrangements to be there. An invitation should never be an afterthought.

You should associate yourself with ambitious, hard-working individuals. If you decide to have friends who chase women 24–7, or constantly partake in activities that aren't productive, then this will probably be your destiny. Surround yourself with individuals who push you to work and grind harder. Their work ethic provides the motivation for you to push harder. We all try to fit in with our friends one way or the other, so you might as well want to fit in with positive-minded people.

Friends should be uplifting. This doesn't mean they tell you what you want to hear, but if you have friends who never have anything positive to say, then you should distance yourself immediately. This could be because they look upon the friendship as a competition more than a friendship. A friendship should never be a competition over who has or is doing what.

Using your friend for inspiration isn't about competing against them. The worst part about these friends is that they tend to always have something negative to say. This is their way of downplaying your accomplishments.

This is a dead giveaway for jealousy. Having a jealous friend is detrimental to your mental peace of mind. When they say or do something that is a sign of jealousy it can literally throw off the rest of your evening or even longer, in some cases. So instead of putting your energy toward something positive, you're letting this individual's negative energy zap and drain you of your energy which could have been used to focus on your purpose.

There's a saying that you won't know who your true friends are until a time of need comes. True friends will always be there for you when you're in a crisis. Anybody can be there for you when things are good, but there are not a lot of individuals that will be there for you when you really need them.

For instance, if you have a friend that you didn't hear from when your transmission on your car went out, but before that, you would hear from them constantly to come pick them up. This is an individual who only values what you can do for them.

In life, there will always be ups and downs. You are bound to have another situation where you need your friend to have your back again, but nothing will change. They've already shown you their true colors. When someone shows you their true colors, you should take heed and act accordingly.

You can always tell if someone is a loyal individual by how they talk about other friends of theirs when they're not around. If they do this, then it's a very good chance they'll talk about you when you're not around.

Make sure to surround yourself with trustworthy friends because we trust friends with a lot of personal information, and you don't want to have friends that betray that trust in them. You shouldn't trust too many people completely to begin with, but if you tell the wrong friend something very personal, it can have ongoing lasting consequences.

When to Start Investing

There are a lot of smart financial people in the world who will tell you not to pay off debt if you have an interest rate below 5 percent. Their rationale behind this is that you can get a much higher return in pretty much any other investment you engage in, like real estate and the stock market.

My issue with this practice is that it leaves you vulnerable to *risk*. Risk is something that a lot of individuals don't take into consideration when investing. The fact of the matter is that people forget that when you're investing your money, it's still a gamble, no matter how you slice it. There's no surefire way to invest to guarantee seeing a return.

Now historically, the stock market and housing market have always had their ups and downs, but they've always rebounded. There's nothing that indicates this will ever change, but remember this: everything always happened until the day it didn't.

I say this not to frighten you away from investing but to let you know there is no such thing as a sure thing when it comes to investment. They all come with some type of risk, some with more than others, but nonetheless it's still a risk. The higher the risk the bigger the return.

You should try to make sure that your financial situation is built upon a solid footing. When you're overleveraging, you're seriously putting your financial situation at great risk. How I look at leveraging is if you can't afford the bank payments yourself without any tenants, then don't do it.

Let's assume you have three mortgages as investments. The way I look at it is if you can't afford to pay the mortgages void of any tenants, you're overleveraged. A lot of banks don't care if you've overleveraged yourself. When you invest and you have no debt, you allow your investment to grow and don't put yourself in a situation where you have to sell assets before they can mature—or even worse, when your investment's market is at a low point.

When you make investments, you're thinking long-term, which means you're prepared for ups and downs in your investment's market, but let's say your financial situation isn't on solid ground, and you lose your job. Now, since you have debt and not a great savings, you end up having to sell assets when your investments market is not in a good place.

No big deal, if you don't need it, because it'll probably go back up over time, but it's terrible news if you're in a pinch for money. So you end up selling assets at a loss.

Another factor most individuals don't bring into the equation is stress. When your financial situation is built on quicksand, your mental state is in constant flux. Be prepared to have a few sleepless nights due to the amount of stress you're bringing upon yourself. When your financial situation is built on quicksand, you know in the back of your head that with any obstacles that life seems to throw your way, when you're the least prepared for it, you could lose everything.

Whatever difference you're making by investing instead of paying off the debt is not worth it on the stress aspect alone. A good night's sleep is invaluable to me.

Credit

Having good credit is virtually essential in today's world unless you have the cash to buy everything outright. That little three-digit number score has a big impact on your lifestyle. That score can be the difference between you getting a great interest rate or a subprime interest rate.

For instance, a guy with an 800 credit score could get an interest rate of 3 percent or lower, while another guy with a credit score below 600 will probably be hit with the subprime rate of 16 percent or more.

This difference in interest rates could cost you hundreds of dollars a month in interest fees. That's money you could be using to invest for your future. You should only get cars that the ROI from long-term investments can purchase. You should never purchase cars with active income.

You have to train yourself to acquire assets first; then you can buy liabilities, if you so choose to, down the road. To qualify for the better interest rates, you have to clean up your credit situation. The first thing I would do is get a credit report to see if you have any delinquent or derogatory items on your credit report. You can get one free credit report a year from annualcreditreport.com.

If you have some items that are delinquent or derogatory, I recommend trying to get in contact with whomever has listed you as delinquent or with derogatory items. See if you can set up some kind of payment plan, and see if they'll settle for less money, or even pay it in full if you have the money on hand.

If it's close to the seven-year mark, then you probably can just let it just expire from your credit report. A derogatory item expires after seven years. Sometimes, you can just dispute the claim and solve it that way.

Nobody said you're going to have an 800 credit score overnight. If you have a wrecked credit report this is going to be a long and tedious process. You didn't screw your credit up overnight, so you won't fix it overnight.

After you've contacted whomever had you in the delinquent or derogatory category and got that handled, I recommend getting a secured credit card. Secured cards are easier to obtain because you're securing it with your own money.

Avoid fee-harvester cards that charge you a monthly maintenance fee. Fee-harvester cards target individuals with bad credit because they know you're desperate for credit. While these cards do build credit since they report to the credit bureaus, they're just not the best option available. There are plenty of banks that offer secured credit cards, but I went with Capitol One.

The goal here is to pay at least the monthly minimum every month, since paying on time is one of the biggest factors when calculating your credit score. Credit utilization is another high factor when calculating your credit score, but ideally this is something you should concern yourself with when you're actually about to use your credit to purchase something. Credit utilization is the percentage of credit you've used minus what you have available.

For example, let's say you have a $1,000 credit card and you've spent $300 on this card. Your utilization would be 30 percent. Most experts advise individuals to not go over this 30 percent mark because that keeps you in the good category as far as utilization. If you go beyond this 30 percent mark, you leave that good category as far as utilization goes your score will be impacted dramatically.

Ideally, you don't want to buy items you can't pay off each month. Living within your means is always the best approach when acquiring financial and mental peace. Over time, your credit score will gradually improve, as long as you pay on time and keep your utilization in check.

After about a year, most secure cards upgrade you from your secured credit card to a regular card. This means they will give you back your security deposit. They may even upgrade you to a cash back card. A cash back card is a card that gives you money back every time you make a purchase. These cards' cash back offers can range anywhere from cash back to airline miles. The airline miles cards are usually reserved for higher credit scores though.

If you decide to dabble in real estate down the road, a good credit score can help you have a better cash flow. Cash flow is the profit you make from an investment each month. For example, if you have a rental property with a mortgage of $800, but you're able to rent it out for $1,300 a month, then you have a cash flow of $500 a month on this rental property. That has to include all expenses on the property like taxes, insurance, maintenance etc.

If you're paying a higher mortgage due to a bad credit score, this will kill your cash flow due to the fact your margin between what you're paying in mortgage and what you're able to charge for rent will be drastically reduced. It could still, in most cases, be a great investment due to the appreciation value, but you want the cash flow also.

Cash flow is key if you're seeking financial freedom because it's the cash flow from investments that provide the all-important financial freedom. Nothing is wrong with getting the appreciation value, but there's nothing wrong with a little cash flow also while you're at it. Besides, your tenant is paying down the mortgage.

If you're not responsible with credit cards, then you should avoid them altogether. Some people just handle having money at their disposal and not spending it. I don't have that problem, but I'm not here to judge anyone, so if this is a problem of yours, then it's probably in your best interest to build your credit another way.

I'll say this though: how can you ever expect to obtain financial freedom if you have no self-control? That's like a fat man trying to lose weight with no self-control over food. If the thought of having excess cash in your bank account causes you to feel like you have to spend it, then you'll never obtain financial freedom. You have to get rid of those demons first.

To obtain financial freedom you have to start thinking like an adult and lose that impulsiveness. I recommend giving yourself a reward system in the same way a person gives themselves a cheat day. Every time you accomplish a major feat, you reward yourself with a small shopping spree. This not only keeps you from overspending, but it also serves as a great motivator when you're trying to get something done. It's very easy for me to stick to my diet when I know I can eat whatever I want on the weekend.

How to Invest

You should start investing as soon as you've eliminated all debt. I prefer to do it this way because it puts my financial situation on solid ground. The sooner you can start investing, the more you can take advantage of compounding interest.

Compound interest is when you take advantage of adding interest to your principle amount invested plus the interest already added. For example, if you've invested $10,000 into the stock market and got a 6 percent return on that investment in a year, that would mean that your new balance is $10,600.

Let's assume you get that same 6 percent return on investment next year. This means that 6 percent would be added to the $10,600, not the just the principle amount of $10,000. This is, of course, if you don't take dividend payouts. Dividends is the interest payout from companies to their shareholders.

For example, let's assume that instead of letting your interest compound, you decided to take quarterly dividend payments. This means that every three months, you would receive a dividend payment of approximately $150. This is hypothetically speaking, because maybe the markets were down the first half of the year, and you obtained that 6 percent return in the latter part of the year. Compound interest done over many years and decades can add up very quickly.

A common way most experts advise to invest is to invest aggressively if you're younger, and go with a more conservative approach as you get closer to retirement. This means that you invest in more stocks when you're young and gradually move toward more bonds as you get older.

Stocks are more volatile than bonds. I don't have time to watch the Dow Jones and read businesses progress reports all day, so I just invest in the market as a whole, as most mutual fund investors never beat the market anyway. I don't believe in speculating, as it's more of a short-term mind-set. Speculating is when you try to time the market. Timing the market is when you try to buy and sell stocks according to market value. I'm more of a long-term investor, and in it for the long haul.

There's an investment strategy called the three-fund portfolio that most financial investors suggest if you're trying to buy index funds for long-term growth. This portfolio usually consists of a domestic stock total market index fund, an international stock total market index fund, and a bond total market index fund.

I prefer using a four-fund portfolio. That means that I invest in all of the aforementioned funds, but I also invest in an index fund that covers just the Standard & Poor's (S&P) 500. The S&P 500 doesn't cover the entire US stock market like a total market index fund. It just covers the top 500 companies in the United States. This means that it comes with a slightly higher risk. The S&P 500 has a solid track record over the long haul as a good investment for passive income.

The issue is most people get frightened if they see the market drop for a couple of days, and then they sell. You can't expect to take advantage of that sweet compounding interest if you're frightened every time the market dips. You can buy mutual funds and let an investor handle your money for you with a small commission and fee, of course.

I just invest in index funds with Vanguard. Vanguard has some of the best expense ratios, but there are plenty of stock brokerage companies like Fidelity, Merrill Lynch, Charles Schwab, etc. Do some homework and find out which company suits you best. Index funds are a good way to make passive income, as it's totally passive and requires no trading and selling.

Of course, you can go with mutual funds, but my only issue with those are that they cost a lot more money in fees and investors rarely can beat the market. Even if you found a broker who could beat the market, by the time you factor in fees, you actually made less. The Vanguard index funds I invest in are the Vanguard Total

Stock Market Index Fund Admiral Shares (VTSAX), the Vanguard Total International Stock Index Fund Admiral Shares (VTIAX), the Vanguard Total Bond Market Index Fund Admiral Shares (VBTLX), and the Vanguard 500 Index Fund Admiral Shares (VFIAX).

You should have a Roth or traditional IRA if you're self-employed or if your job doesn't offer a 401(k). I have a Roth IRA because when I take my money out in my sixties, I want it to be tax-free. I'm more of a delayed gratification person. That means I don't mind paying now to have more later.

Investments

The best investment you can make is into yourself. This simply means you spent money acquiring a skill, an education, or some sort of knowledge that will last a lifetime.

A lot of people debate whether going into debt worth getting a college education. It isn't, if you don't take the time out and research the field you're pursuing to see what the market is paying for that field. If you obtain the right education that pays a great salary, then this is what I would call good debt.

No way am I implying that a college education is the only way to obtain success, but it doesn't hurt either, especially if you haven't discovered what you have a passion for. Once you're making your desired salary, then you should try to pay off any debt with that salary. If this means you live a little frugally then that's what you have to do.

Once you've gotten rid of all your debt, then it's time to start investing. Real estate, stocks, bonds, or a business are some great investments, just to name a few. If you don't make enough money to invest, then I suggest investing into acquiring more skills to enhance your income. You should make sure your active income is substantial enough first before you start investing. You need a strong cash cow to fund your investments. If you're content with just making minimal investments into the stock market, then I guess that's a personal decision, but I suggest investing that money into acquiring more skills to achieve more active income.

While passive income is the key to financial freedom, it is, however, very minimal returns initially compared to a solid cash cow. For instance, if you have a high-paying skill that pays a $100,000 a year, do you have any idea how many rental properties you would need to have to make a $100,000 passively?

For example, let's assume you buy homes in the $100,000 range. Let's then assume you get approved for a 3.5 percent interest rate on those homes after putting down 20 percent to avoid the private mortgage insurance (PMI) rate. Let's them assume you're able to create $400 of cash flow from each home after all expenses. This is a lofty goal, but this is just an example. To make that same $100,000, you would need to have approximately twenty rental properties. That would then mean that you needed over $400,000 to put down the 20 percent needed to avoid the PMI.

It takes even more money to create that $100,000 in the stock market. For hypothetical reasons, let's just assume the stock market gives you a return of 10 percent a year. This is again a very lofty goal, but for this example, let's just go with it. If the stock market gave you a 10 percent return annually, that would mean you had to have $1 million invested into the stock market to acquire that same income.

The goal here isn't to dissuade anyone from investing into real estate or the stock market, but I'm simply trying to inform you that your best investment is always in yourself. A high-paying skill or education will, in most cases, give you better returns on investment.

Real estate takes a little work when you start, but it can become passive once you've gotten everything taken care of. By taken care of, I'm referring to doing any repair on the property, if needed, and finding a reliable tenant who's going to pay the rent on time and not destroy your property. Even then, it's not 100 percent passive unless you decide to hire a property manager to manage the property for a small fee. A lot of property managing companies prefer for you to have a certain amount of properties to be eligible for this service.

Stocks and bonds can be passive if you invest in index funds that follow the entire stock market. Of course, you can engage in day trading or things of the sort that require constant attention to the market. Either one of these investments can bring you anywhere from 5 percent to over 20 percent interest if you're lucky.

Of course, there are no guarantees with anything. The housing and the stock market have both crashed before, but the good news is that they have always recovered. Buying index funds with Vanguard admiral package start at $3,000. If the $3,000 price tag is too lofty for you, I suggest investing whatever you have into acquiring more skills. You'll get a better rate of return.

You can always buy individual stocks, but this is riskier, in my opinion. Buying index funds that comprise the entire stock market offer you much better protection in my book. If a couple of businesses are tanking, then there are others that can more than make up for it.

If real estate is your thing, then you can use leverage to acquire a property. Leverage is when you use debt to make money. This is commonly referred to as good debt. I'm not big on credit unless it's to acquire an education or skill, but that's a decision you have to make for yourself. If you do use leverage, just make sure your active income can cover your mortgages.

For most, using debt is the only way they can acquire real estate property. If you decide to go this route, I recommend putting 20 percent down for the property to avoid paying PMI. PMI is required anytime you put less than 20 percent down on a property. If you're paying PMI, that would greatly reduce your cash flow, if not kill it altogether.

Remember, you can still make money off of appreciation, but cash flow is always a positive. You always have government-assisted loans like FHA that only require as little as 3.5 percent. If you don't mind buying rural property, you can get an USDA loan with zero dollars down if you meet certain income requirements. You have other options that also require nothing down. Just understand that this just means you'll pay more on a monthly basis for your mortgage.

Another thing to consider is that most banks prefer this property to be your primary residence. Another great way to invest your money is by starting your own business, or if you already have your own business, you can reinvest some of savings into growing the business-like marketing. If you have a restaurant or bar you could upgrade the interior to make it more aesthetically pleasing. Of course, the old phrase "if it ain't broke, don't fix it" can be very true in most cases.

Know What You're Investing In

People, for the most part, are lazy individuals who are looking for the quick fix. When you're looking to invest your hard-earned money, make sure you're doing your due diligence to research what you're looking to invest in.

If you're looking to invest in real estate, make sure you know if the property is losing value or gaining value. Is the neighborhood on the uptick or is crime starting to trickle into the neighborhood? Try checking some crime statistics of the area, if available. Is it decreasing or increasing? Check to see what the property value was ten years ago. Has it gone up or has it gone down? You don't want to buy property that's depreciating.

A lot of people run out and buy stocks without doing an ounce of research when they hear how good the stock is doing in the market. Then they're sick to their stomach the next month when the stock is plummeting. If you're going to invest in stocks and bonds you should be in them for the long haul anyway, in my opinion, but you definitely want to make sure you check the track record of said stock.

I don't like the emotional rollercoaster of investing in individual stocks as is. That's why I prefer to buy index funds that allow me to buy stocks in the stock market as a whole. Do not put your money into an investment that your friend told you was doing well, or a co-worker convinced you to buy a property because the area is supposedly on the uptick. More than likely, they heard it from a third party and were just repeating what they heard. Not exactly reliable expert advice.

Always do your own homework before investing your hard-earned money.

Dress for Success

Making a great first impression is critical when trying to close a sale or when you're applying for that job you've been wanting. A major component to making this great impression is your attire.

I vividly remember applying for a security job in New York City when I first arrived. I was thinking, "Hey, this is just a measly security job. What do they expect, an Armani suit?"

Well, to my surprise, when I arrived there all the other guys who were applying had on slacks, dress shoes, and button up shirts. Meanwhile, I had on jeans, a T-shirt, and tennis shoes.

The guy giving the interview called us each in one at a time. He interviewed the other guys for about ten minutes, while he only interviewed me for what felt like ten seconds. I'm quite sure he was thinking, "Why would I give a guy a job who is not even taking the job interview seriously?" I think he kept my interview short because he wanted to give me the same amount of time that I put in to prepare for the interview.

Needless to say, I didn't get the job. Do I think that I would've gotten the job if I had spent more time on my appearance? Maybe or maybe not. Who knows? But what I do know is that it couldn't have hurt. I didn't put myself in the best position possible.

I had an opportunity to redeem myself when I applied for a personal trainer position a couple years later. I wore a suit for this interview, and I got the job. Did I get this job based solely on my suit? Maybe or maybe not, but what I do know is that I gave the impression of someone who was taking this opportunity seriously.

Right or wrong, humans make a snap judgement about you from the first few seconds they lay eyes on you. You don't have to wear a tailored Armani suit to impress potential clients or employers. In fact, that could be too much, depending on what you're doing. What I've found to be a good, happy medium are some slacks, dress shoes, and a button up dress shirt tucked in. You can substitute the slacks for jeans, if you want; just make sure they have no logos or anything like that on them. If you're a female, a nice dress that's not too form-fitting should suffice. It should be fitted, though, just not overdone.

Remember you lose or gain a lot of business the first few seconds someone lays eyes on you.

Intuition

Listening to your intuition can be one of your biggest assets in life, but there are times when it can actually hinder you. For instance, when you start to pursue your purpose, and you come to a crossroads as to whether you should quit your job and pursue your purpose in life full-time, your intuition will be telling you to play it safe. Your intuition—or, as it's commonly referred to, "your gut"—doesn't like to take chances.

When you're taking your life savings to start a business, your intuition will kick in and try to talk you out of your idea. Make no mistake about it, when you're doing any kind of investing, it's all a gamble. I don't care how confident you are in your abilities, it's still a gamble. There are no concrete guaranteed investments. To be clear, some are less risky than others, but it's still a risk, nonetheless.

Also, the lower the risk, the lower the upside, and the higher the risk, the higher the upside. I'm not telling you to never listen to your intuition, but listening to one's intuition is what keeps individuals paralyzed with fear at a dead-end job they hate without ever exploring other opportunities.

When I relocated to New York my intuition was asking me, "Are you crazy?" I had no support system in New York and very little money saved. A lot of people live in small towns with very little opportunity, and they're afraid to leave because their intuition talks them out of it.

Now I'm not suggesting that someone just up and packs to move to a bigger city on a whim. If you decide to make a decision to move to a bigger city, it should be done with months of planning in advance. Even then, your intuition probably will be kicking in to discourage you. "Play it safe," your intuition will tell you.

If you want to live the life you've always wanted to live, you will have to get accustomed to discomfort. If you decide to invest into the stock market, your intuition will want you to just play it safe and put it in your savings account. There's a reason only a select few live the life they truly want to live, and that's because they're the only ones strong enough mentally to not play it safe and take a chance, but for every entrepreneur who beat the odds and is living their dreams, there are a hundred that crashed and burned.

With that being said, I would rather crash and burn knowing that I gave it a try than go through life with regret from never even trying. I can live with defeat, but I can't live with the fear of never trying.

Lifestyle

If you want to accomplish your goals, you're going to need a lot of energy. Thus you must live a healthy lifestyle. When I eat junk food, it makes me feel lethargic. As the old saying goes, "Health is wealth." I've found this to be very true in my own life.

You can have all the money in world, but if you're ailing or sick, you won't enjoy it much. I guess the money is good for getting the best healthcare available, but you should also want to spend it doing the things you love. A healthy diet and consistent exercise routine should be in every aspiring entrepreneur's weekly routine.

While I'm all for pursuing your passion in life, it should not come at the expense of neglecting your health. A lot of entrepreneurs or would-be entrepreneurs get so caught up in building their empire that their health takes a backseat.

When you're an entrepreneur, your schedule is hectic, so the only way to get the proper nutrition and exercise is to prioritize it. That means when you make your schedule or routine out for the week, you've made time to prepare your meals and exercise. If you're a busy individual, then asking you to prepare five meals a day and commit to a one-hour workout four to five days a week may be a tad unreasonable, but to be honest, it doesn't take all that to stay healthy.

You can try to meal prep on Sunday for Monday through Wednesday, then prep meals on Wednesday evening for Thursday and Friday. That's only two days you've spent on meal preparation. Not much of a sacrifice, if you think about it. You can even try eating out, as best you can, if two days of meal prep is still too much. Subway, Chipotle, and salad locations like Sweetgreen or Chopt are available, to just name a few. Eating out can get very pricey, so if cash flow is an issue, then the two days of meal prep may be the only option available.

As far as working out goes just remember you're not trying to win Mr. Olympia or the Arnold Classic. You're just trying to stay tight and fit. You don't need an hour workout five days a week to accomplish this.

Three thirty-minute workouts a week done in a circuit training style to get the heart rate up should accomplish this. Technically, you don't even need a gym. This can be accomplished at home. All you need is a couple of adjustable dumbbells.

A simple routine to follow for a busy individual would be pushups, immediately followed by dumbbell rows, followed by dumbbell reverse lunges, followed by crunches, followed by dumbbell curls, followed by overhead tricep extensions. If done this way, you can kill two birds with one stone—strength training and cardiovascular training done simultaneously. I would rest approximately two to three minutes and repeat. I would do this about three or four times, depending on fitness level.

If done three times a week, combined with a healthy diet full of lean proteins, fruits, vegetables, and healthy fats, it should be more than enough to stay lean and healthy.

Dealing with Haters

You should expect to encounter jealousy on your path to financial freedom. The hardest part of jealousy is when it comes from friends and loved ones. It's mentally tough dealing with haters, no matter where it comes from, but it's ten times more difficult when it's coming from a family member or lifelong friend.

When we accomplish things or feats in life, we all like to tell our relatives or close friends, thinking they'll be happy or proud of us, but more times than not, if you look closely, there's some hidden envy going on. We all have family and close friends that are genuinely happy for us, but for some of us, the overwhelming majority of us can expect to see withdrawal from some of our family members and inner circle, unless they've achieved some similar type of success.

In some cases, even if they've experienced some resemblance of your success or accomplishment, they're still not genuinely happy for you because they liked the idea of having more success than you. I would start to distance myself from individuals who displayed this type of behavior toward my success, even if it was a close friend or family member. The reason I would do this is because that negative energy would start to drain you and probably start to weigh on your mind throughout the day. Instead of applying your energy for positive things like growing your business or whatever you're trying to accomplish, you'll spend your day wondering why your friends have an attitude toward you.

If you want to truly accomplish financial and mental peace, you have to get comfortable with cutting people out of your life. To accomplish true financial and mental peace, you have to have an abundance mind-set in every area of your life. That means you have an abundance mind-set with your dating life, jobs, clients, and loved ones.

It has been said that family can be the fastest ones to bring you down, and I've found this to be true for the most part. As far as the haters outside of family and friends, you just need to understand they're admirers who don't know how to display their affection for you. Kind of like the girl who liked you in elementary school, but she didn't know how to tell you she liked you, so she hit you instead.

Look at it this way, if you're not accomplishing anything, you wouldn't have any haters. Having haters should be an indication you're doing something right. Nobody hates on the homeless man who sleeps in the park. If I don't have any haters, I feel like I'm doing something wrong. Use haters as a barometer of your success. The more haters, the more success you're encountering.

Don't encourage hating by blatantly bragging or boasting. Let your accomplishments speak for themselves. No need to throw them in everyone's face every chance you get. This doesn't mean you can't go buy that luxury item you've been wanting so you don't hurt anyone's feelings. If individuals are going to get in their feelings because you've bought an item you've worked hard and sacrificed for, then that's on them.

What I'm saying is that you don't have to brag to them about how much you paid for it unless they ask. Even then you could say, "I'm keeping that to myself" to display some form of modesty.

Being humble and modest can kill a lot of jealousy, but at the end of the day, there's no foolproof way to kill all jealousy. Expect haters to lie or do whatever they can to bring you down. Simply pay it no mind because you'll only give them satisfaction if they know they got under your skin. Envy and jealousy are just a part of human nature, and quite frankly, I don't ever think that's changing.

Don't Be a Hater

It takes a lot more energy to be negative than it does to be positive. It takes more face muscles to frown than it does to smile. There's a reason that haters rarely ever accomplish anything. It's because they spend most of their free time hating on others.

Hating is a full-time job with no fringe benefits. When you're a hater, you spend your time occupied with what someone else is accomplishing instead of using that energy for productivity. Instead of finding ways to accomplish your goals, you're watching their social media pages, and you're filled with jealousy and envy.

There's nothing wrong with wanting what others have, and to be honest that's quite natural, but use that desire to motivate you to try and strive harder for what you're trying to accomplish or want, not for jealousy.

My motto is "the same way they got it, I can go get it." Learn to be a genuine congratulator and let others' achievements motivate you, not discourage you—or even worse, become a vessel of negativity. Notice I used the phrase *genuine congratulator*. That's because a lot of individuals will congratulate you, but it's not coming from a place of genuine happiness for others. This negative energy you're putting into the universe is what you get back in return.

Also, when you're a hater, friends of yours might start distancing themselves to avoid the negative energy you bring with you. Nobody likes to spend their free time with negative people. Just keep in mind that for anything someone else accomplishes, you can accomplish those same goals if you dedicate yourself to accomplishing them.

Social Anxiety

The human need to fit in has been around since the beginning of time. We are social creatures, so our need of acceptance is something no human can deny.

Social anxiety, in most cases, should be treated by a medical professional, but I'll tell you how I conquered my social anxiety. I was very shy when I was younger, which I believe is a direct correlation to social anxiety. My shyness stemmed from the fear of awkwardness, and therefore, I felt like the less I said the better. It wasn't until I accepted the fact that some people would like me and others wouldn't that I started getting over my shyness. It's as simple as that, the world is not designed for every individual to be liked by everyone.

In the dating world, some people of the opposite sex are going to find you attractive while others aren't. There's no such thing as a universal beauty. Looks are subjective, and so is likability. Just be yourself, and those who don't like you—oh, well.

A lot of people's insecurities stem from the fact that they just don't have this simple yet difficult understanding of human interactions. To put it simply, *not everybody is going to like you*! You might as well be yourself and concern yourself with individuals who like you for who you are, and damn the rest.

No matter how cool you are, someone's going to dislike you. No matter how smooth you are, someone's going to dislike you. No matter how charming you are, someone's going to dislike you. The all-important abundance mind-set reigns supreme once again. Are you starting to notice a trend?

Until you develop an abundance mind-set you will always be a prisoner in your own mind. A mind that lives in scarcity will always be controlled by rejection. Rejection is just a part of human interaction. The individuals that accept it, but don't let it determine their worth, are the individuals who will obtain the mate of their dreams, the social circle they desire, and the business they want. To obtain any of those an abundance mind-set is required, because you have to go through a lot of rejections and failures to obtain that mate, circle of friends, or business you truly want.

I'm no longer shy because I couldn't care less about who likes me as an individual. I'm just myself, and anyone who doesn't like it doesn't have to be in my life, simple as that. Now, I'm well aware that any anxiety you might have could be serious, and you should probably seek medical attention, but I wanted to give you a quick tip on how I overcame my anxiety.

Abundance Mind-Set

When I was a teenager, my friends and I would hit the local shopping mall to approach women. It was during this time period that I developed my abundance mind-set.

When my friends and I would approach women, I noticed something that would change my mind-set for the rest of my life. I noticed I would get some women's number, while others would reject me.

I quickly realized that it simply was a numbers game. The more women I approached, the more numbers I would get. I also noticed something else in stark contrast to approaching women at the mall. Whenever I would stop going to the mall to approach women, my Saturday nights would always be available, meaning I had no date. If you're a fisherman, you can't expect to catch any fish if you never throw your line into the water.

Oddly enough the more I got rejected, the less they would bother me until they stopped bothering me altogether. I simply realized that it was impossible for every woman to find me attractive or be available at that moment, and by available, I mean she's not talking to anyone, she's not emotionally available, or she has no time to date. This was critical for me to understand this because this allowed me to not take a rejection personally, but also to take into account other factors at play.

When you're trying to get someone's business, you must understand that a rejection is not a rejection to you directly. Timing is the biggest component when it comes down to getting a woman's number or a potential client's business.

Maybe financially, they're not in a position to do business with you at the moment. Maybe they have a lot on their plate businesswise at the moment, and right now is not the right time schedulewise.

When I was a trainer at the gym, I would get rejected a lot, but that never stopped me from approaching potential new clients. Some of the leads would tell me about how often they were approached on the floor. I would ask them why they decided to train with me when they had already been approached by other trainers on the floor, and the universal answer would always be *timing*.

Whether it was activities going on with their kids, financial situation not being where they wanted it to be or heavy work load the timing just wasn't right. I simply approached them at the right time. Had I approached them a week earlier or a week later, I might've gotten rejected.

Never take rejections personally. It'll only dampen your confidence. Individuals with an abundance mind-set have the understanding that *timing*, and not them directly, is largely the reason for rejection. An abundance mind-set is required in life to obtain anything worth obtaining. If it was easy to obtain, then everybody would obtain it.

How to Develop Thick Skin

If you're a public figure like myself, you're going to have to develop some type of thick skin to deal with the scrutiny that comes along with being in the public eye.

As a public figure, once you get popular enough, people use your name for clickbait to attract eyeballs to your video, article, or social media posting. This is why you see a lot of kids who were stars on television when they were younger totally disappear from the public scene. Now, it goes without saying that most of them probably just couldn't get another job in the industry, but some of them just didn't want to deal with the scrutiny that comes along with being in the public eye.

Unfortunately, you don't have to be a public figure to encounter scrutiny. Your peers, co-workers, employers, family members, and friends can all criticize you. When I started doing YouTube videos, I would read every comment and watch every reaction video about me and try to brush it off, but I quickly realized that I'm a human being with emotions just like everyone else, and some of the things said about me really got me upset.

Every day I would type "Alpha Male Strategies" into the YouTube search bar to see if someone made another disparaging video about me. I quickly realized that I was the one bringing stress upon myself by actively seeking out negativity. Unless you're an alien or an emotionless sociopath, negative things being said about you are going to bother you. It's impossible to develop thick skin, so to speak, so the secret to developing thick skin is to not have to develop the thick skin to begin with.

Let me explain. The problem was I was actively looking for negativity when, in actuality, I should have been ignoring it all together. And by ignoring, I'm referring to not actively seeking negativity. I was looking for negativity; therefore, I found negativity.

Once you learn to ignore the negativity or scrutiny coming your way, the more peaceful your life will become. I soon stopped looking for negativity surrounding me. If a subscriber of mine on YouTube would try to inform me of another YouTuber making videos or comments about me, I simply blocked the subscriber from my channel because they were trying to bring negativity into my life.

You may not be a popular YouTuber, but this happens in the real world also when a friend informs you of someone supposedly saying something negative about you behind your back. They are purposely trying to bring negativity into your life. In real life, you don't have a block button to block people out of your life, but the same rules apply. You should block them out of your life, or at the very least pull back from them a bit.

If you work a job where there is constant negativity surrounding the job, and it's leaving you stressed out at the end of the day, you have to ask yourself, "Why are you still working there?" That's the epitome of having a scarcity mind-set.

Don't get me wrong; I'm well aware that you may have responsibilities, so I'm not suggesting you quit your job on a whim, but you should be preparing yourself in the time being, or better yet, looking for another job to replace that one if starting your own business isn't an option financially at the moment.

Learn to disassociate yourself from anything or anyone who brings negativity into your life, and there will be no need to develop thick skin because, in actuality, there isn't a way to develop it anyway.

Your favorite entertainers get killed daily from talk shows, bloggers, radio shows, and social media followers. To deal with that type of constant criticism, they simply have to not watch or listen to it.

Have you seen some of the comments on Instagram of some of your favorite celebrities? The comments are horrible and would probably stress the celebrity out if they actually read them. This is why most celebrities either don't read their comments, or they pay someone to control their social media activity. You won't be able to obtain your goals if you're easily sidetracked by criticism.

Evolving

There's a saying in business that I've found to be extremely true: If you aren't growing, you're dying. In business, stagnation is the first sign you need to change things up. This is why you see clubs packed for a few months, and then their patrons grow tired of the same old routine and slowly stop coming to support. Humans are peculiar beings. We need constant change to keep us stimulated.

This doesn't hold true in our daily routine, as we typically follow the same routine throughout the workweek, but when it comes to our source of entertainment, we tend to like to try different things after a while.

When I first started out as a full-time personal trainer, I lost clients at an alarming rate at the beginning. I soon realized the reason behind this: the clients simply grew tired of doing the same routine after a while. They liked me and all, but at some point, they had to come to the conclusion that they could do it on their own and save the enormous amount of money a personal trainer in Manhattan cost.

To counteract this, I simply enhanced my skills as a trainer. Before, I only focused on barbell and dumbbell workouts. Now I would be a trainer who specialized in workouts with kettlebells, bosu balls, landmines, medicine balls, sliders, cables, machines, ViPR, etc.

Once I advanced my training capabilities, my retention rate skyrocketed. I learned to evolve my clients' programs constantly to stave off program boredom. This subtle but very valuable change allowed me to maintain my clients longer, which allowed me to make more money.

This is why growth is important because if you gain a client, but at the same time, you lose a client, you haven't made any progress. If you had maintained your previous client, combined with your new client, you would be making some headway. So if you're running a business, you can't expect your business to grow if for every new customer you get you lose an old customer. Evolution is the key to survival in any business.

When you invest in a stock, you're basically investing your money into a company that you think will evolve their business enough that they continue to grow, or if the stock is down and you buy stocks into the company your reasoning behind making that investment is that you're betting the company would figure it out and turn things around.

Of course, some companies never do, and you lose money, or companies that were once winning bets lose momentum. Keep in mind that down stock may very well get their momentum back. You can avoid all this headache if you invested in index funds due to the stock variety. Index funds do lose value, but they're much more likely to turn things around, as opposed to individual stocks.

You have to keep up with the latest trends in business, and if your competition is getting more business than you, it might be smart to try and analyze what they're doing. Maybe you can adopt some of things they're implementing that make them so successful.

Investing and Spending Are Both Habit Forming

Spending money can be very addictive. I've known individuals who work hard all week, only to blow it all in the mall on Friday. Now, it's not up to me to tell someone how to spend the money they worked hard for. People are free to spend their money any way they see fit, but my issue is when these same people will then turn right around and blame *The Man* for their financial shortcomings. Not everyone, of course, but some would.

Losing that consumer mind-set is very hard for some people to do, as shopping and spending money releases the happy endorphins akin to an overweight individual eating fattening food. Although both of these addictions are hard to break, they both can be done with some self-restraint, if one is truly desiring to change their life around. The key is to take baby steps toward beating the addiction.

When most overweight individuals decide to lose weight or adopt a healthier lifestyle, usually start going to the gym two hours on six days a week and cut most of their calories out of their diet. This usually doesn't last long, however, as the body has a hard time with drastic change in a short period of time. Not only will your body be incredibly sore from the extreme workload from the gym, without building up the physical tolerance needed to handle that kind of workout, but your body will start craving sugar, since you're in such a calorie deficit, causing you to break your diet. The proper approach would have been to start working out three days a week, with thirty minutes at each workout, and gradually increase your duration or intensity in the gym.

The same holds true for the diet. Instead of cutting your calories low enough that a mouse would starve, you would have been better off cutting your calories down only 20 percent from maintenance to stave off hunger pangs.

This is the same kind of approach you should adopt with your spending habit. If you're the type of individual who spends pretty much their entire check on the weekend without saving anything, then try saving $50 each week to start to build your saving muscle. Try to maintain this every week for a month or so.

After you've done this for over a month, try to save a $100 a week to further build your saving muscle. Saving money can become as addictive as spending money. People who are addicted to saving money can come across as cheap to some.

There are extremes in both spectrums, but I would much rather be extreme at saving money rather than spending. I don't want you spending your money before it even touches your hand, but I also don't want you having a million dollars in the bank eating hot dogs and spam, still trying to save more money. In life, you need balance, and you can go too far either way.

After taxes have been deducted from your income, a good spending breakdown can be 20 percent for fun, 30 percent for bills, and 50 percent for investing or saving, preferably investing if you're debt-free with a solid emergency fund. Those percentages aren't an exact science, but you get my point. By fun, I'm referring to clothing and or activities.

If you have to spend more than 30 percent on bills, you might be living beyond your means if you want to have some money to invest. If you're content with your financial situation and not really interested in investing, then obviously your financial breakdown percentages are going to look drastically different.

Investing can be real estate, starting your own business, stocks, bonds, or acquiring an education or skill which I like to refer to as investing in yourself. If you're already an entrepreneur, then you can simply reinvest your profits back into your business.

The irony is that once you've defeated that consumer mind-set, the investment mind-set can become just as addictive. You start to look at money as employees rather than tools for spending. Every dollar I get now is supposed to be making me at least a 5 percent return yearly passively, if invested correctly. This passive income mind-set can become just as addictive because you quickly realize how you can finally escape the rat race and live life on your terms.

Once you have enough money invested to where it can make you enough money passively, you know it's just a matter of time before you're done trading time for money.

Mastering Sales

In business, you'll be hard-pressed to find a bigger component to building a successful business than the ability to sell or close. Most human beings are skeptical creatures by nature, so when someone is trying to sell them something, more times than not, people naturally go into objection mode.

Objections, in sales, are when a potential client or customer tries to throw up a roadblock to your salesmanship. Being a trainer in the city and having to grow my own clientele base from the floor, I can tell you that I've heard it all. The two biggest objections you should grow accustomed to hearing are "I don't know if I have time for that right now" or "I'm not quite sure I can afford it right now. Let me check with my spouse and get back to you."

Yes, lack of money or time will be the biggest objections you're likely to encounter. There are others also, just depending on what you're trying to sell, but those are the two biggest that I've encountered in sales.

You should always have a strategy developed for overcoming each objection. When a potential client would hit me with the old "I'm too busy right now to train," I would immediately amend my approach. I would then inform them I was willing to work around their schedule. My main focus was to get them to buy the sessions, and we could figure the details out later.

You have to understand that if you have a product or service you're offering, you're at the mercy of the customer. They have something you want, which is money, so they have the advantage. Unless you have a product that's highly in demand, everything revolves around the customer's schedule. I wasn't lying to them when I implied I would work around their schedule, but what I understood about clients is that once they grew an attachment to you and liked the results you were getting them, they would be more flexible to your schedule. Of course, they weren't going to do this initially as they're the client and you're the one looking for their business.

When I would hear "I'm not quite sure I can afford it right now," I would immediate change my approach. I would go from trying to sell a twenty-four session training package to trying to sell them a six-session training package. You can't get blood from a turnip, so why even try?

You see this with car dealerships also. If you go to the car lot and ask the price on one vehicle, and you find out it's out of your price range, a good salesman immediately pivots to a more affordable option. A smaller sale is better than no sale.

You can't just assume that someone can afford something just from how they dress or the fact someone is training at an expensive gym. As we all know, most individuals live beyond their means, which means they don't have much, if any, discretionary fund. More times than not, whatever you're trying to sell isn't a life necessity. If that's the case, if you're going to close this sale, you need to make whatever you're offering seem as affordable as possible.

In my situation, instead of trying to get them to train three times a week, I would immediately suggest once a week. I was of the mind-set that once a client could see the value I was bringing to their life, they would start to prioritize my services in their household budget.

Time or money will probably continue to be the biggest objections you encounter, no matter the field, so you should already have your objection tactics ready to go as soon as you hear them.

I want to make something abundantly clear: it won't matter how good you are at overcoming rejections if you're afraid to offer your services. If you're going to build a business, you have to rid yourself of the fear of rejections. Rejections are just a part of the game and you have to just learn how to deal with it. If you never conquer this fear, then it won't matter how good you are overcoming objections if you're afraid to offer your services or business to begin with. If you're still having trouble overcoming objections, you need to try to find a way to show the potential client how your product or service adds value to their life without them actually trying your product or service.

For instance, when I was a trainer and I was trying to sell my services, I would always think of a way I could directly add value to that potential. For example, if I saw a young man on the floor training, and he was between the ages of eighteen and twenty-four, I pretty much knew his primary reason for lifting was for aesthetics. There are not a lot of twenty-year-olds concerned with their cholesterol levels. So when I approached him, I would tell him how many more women I thought he could attract if he invested in me training him and pushing him to the next level.

However, if I approached a fifty-year-old female on the floor, I knew she would care more about health and mobility. Don't get me wrong; I'm quite sure she wanted to look good also, but it's not likely to be at the top of her list for working out.

Once I would approach this older female, I would ask her if she had any pains or discomforts particularly in the lower back, knee, shoulders, or feet areas because I knew these were common areas for muscle imbalances causing joint pain. Then I would let her know that by investing in me to correct these imbalances, she would be a lot more mobile for her grandkids, not to mention free of the discomforts that muscle imbalances bring. This usually triggers a positive response because that's very important as we get older.

The point of all this is you have to find how you can show value for your product or service to the customer, and what brings value to one potential customer's life might not be the same thing that brings value to another potential client's life. This means that if you try to create a cookie cutter approach, it won't be effective because different groups' value systems won't be the same.

Networking

As the saying goes, "Your network determines your net worth." You have to socialize and be liked to network. If you're not a likable person, nobody will want to associate and network with you.

A lot of the breaks given in life were a result of someone knowing someone else. You never know when your success or failure depends on who you know. Maybe you need a specific permit or license, and you know someone who knows someone that can make sure you get all the proper permit or licenses needed for your endeavor.

I don't think there's a person alive who doesn't want to be liked. I think we all can honestly admit this to be true. The problem is you shouldn't try to be liked to fit in with others. That's having a scarcity mind-set, and you should try meeting individuals with your likes and interests. But with that being said, there are some things you can do or stop doing to just be a likable person overall that you might not even be aware you're doing.

Nobody likes a know-it-all type person. This is the individual that tries to tell you everything you're doing wrong in life, when in fact their life situation isn't much better than yours, if any. Try being a better listener and less of a mother or father figure. If someone wanted to get a lecture, they probably would've talked to a parent or a counselor. Sometimes people just want a listening ear without the unsolicited advice all the time.

Sarcastic individuals always love to have a good laugh, but unfortunately, this laugh usually comes at the expense of others. Everyone loves a good laugh, but nobody likes to be the butt of the joke. Learn to keep your sarcastic humor to a minimum.

Everyone loves a humble and modest individual. If you're accomplishing goals, there's no need to remind everyone every five minutes of your accomplishments. It only invites jealousy and envy. Let your accomplishments speak for themselves. Trust me when I say that everyone already knows what you've accomplished.

Encourage people around you. When you're a positive person, people will like to be around you for the positive energy you put into the universe. When you're a positive person, you'll also attract other positive-minded individuals. Now, this doesn't mean you're a butt-kissing pushover; it simply means that you prefer to encourage people instead of tearing them down.

Don't be the type of person who only looks at others for what you can get from them. Friendships should be mutually beneficial. Everyone hates that friend they only hear from when they need something. I usually cut these types of people out of my life immediately.

How Aggressively Should You Invest?

How aggressive someone should have their investment portfolio is going to be based on several factors, but the two most important factors to me are going to be age and risk tolerance. I put age first because no matter what your risk tolerance level, is there's no logical reason a ninety-year-old should have their investment portfolio made up of mostly stocks, in my opinion, unless you're planning to pass them on to your offspring and have no intention of touching that money.

At a certain age you should invest more into bonds than stocks. Yes, stocks have a greater return on investment for your money, but the stock market could be in a downturn in a situation when you're about to retire or in a need for money. I would always have more money invested in stocks because the bond market isn't that much more stable than the stock market, but it is more stable nonetheless.

No matter how down the stock market is, you haven't lost money until you sell your stock. So if you're playing the long game—which is a strategy I advise, by the way, if you're younger—you have ample time for your stocks to rebound if the market takes a dive, but if you're older, you might not have this luxury of waiting for the market to rebound.

If I could go back in time and invest into the stock market as a twenty-five-year-old man just starting to find himself financially, I would undoubtedly invest about 90 percent of my money into stocks. This would be, of course, if I planned to retire at sixty or sixty-five years old. This would give me plenty of time for my stocks to rebound if the stock market hit a low point.

I don't believe in investing in individual stocks because it's rare to find a stockbroker who can beat the market, and they do it for a living, so the odds of me beating it aren't very good. I wholeheartedly believe that anyone investing in the stock market should just buy index funds that cover the entire US and international stock market unless you want to be glued to CNN all day buying and trading stocks like a day trader. Even if you do invest in individual stocks, you're probably better suited to playing the long game even if the stock plummets. I'm being a little facetious there, but you get the point.

So if I were twenty-five years old again, my investment portfolio would comprise of 90 percent stocks and 10 percent bonds. For some individuals, that might be a little too aggressive, but my risk tolerance is pretty high, considering I would be playing the long game.

This should be done, of course, if you have no debt and a nice rainy-day fund. You can't play the long game without a proper savings. If I was thirty-five years old again, I would move to a slightly more conservative approach. I would likely go to a portfolio breakdown of 85 percent stocks and 15 percent bonds. Once again this might be too aggressive for some thirty-five-year-olds, or twenty-five-year-olds for that matter, but my risk tolerance is pretty high. For some this might be too conservative; I guess it just depends on the individual. What's high risk for some might be conservative for others.

Now that I'm approaching forty years old at the time of writing this, my investment portfolio will stay the same as it would if I was thirty-five years old. The reason I wouldn't take a slightly more conservative approach is because I have a nice savings, beyond the typical savings needed for a rainy day, so it's highly likely that I won't need my investment money anytime soon. Of course, you never know when catastrophe could hit, so this is why it's a gamble.

Most people never take risk into account when investing into the stock market because the stock market has a proven track record of over a hundred years of rebounding, no matter how bad it has tanked over its lifetime, but the gamble doesn't come into play as to whether the stock market will make you money over time, if given the chance to rebound in a bad market. That has been proven over and over again.

The gamble comes into play as to whether you'll need the money you've invested in an opportune time when the stock market was at a low point. If you need the money for some unforeseen emergency that your rainy-day fund simply can't cover, you run the risk of having to sell stocks at a loss since you're not in a position to wait for them to rebound.

In my opinion, I can't see a reason for anyone over fifty years old to invest more than 80 percent of their money into stocks unless you have a nice savings, high-paying job, or multiple streams of passive income. If you're an author and you have five books bringing you a sizable income every month, then you might be in a position to invest more aggressively, but unfortunately, this isn't the overwhelmingly majority of people. The average person isn't afforded this luxury.

If it was me living on an average American salary, my investment portfolio would comprise of 75 percent stocks and 25 percent bonds. I know some might disagree with that notion, and you're free to do that, but that's how I would do it.

My biggest issue with investing a lot into bonds is that if interest rates go up, then your bonds lose value since your interest rate of return is already set. This is akin to putting your money into a savings account and inflation decreasing the value of your money over time.

It's All in the Approach

I think we all can agree that rejection is one of the hardest pills to swallow. Abundance mind-set and all, someone telling you flat-out that they're not interested in what you're offering can be a little offsetting to say the least.

As I've mentioned before, timing is probably the biggest component to getting a rejection, but there are other factors that contribute to getting a rejection. Maybe it was your approach, or maybe you had a sandwich with tons of onions and your breath is not exactly minty fresh—who knows. But that's not the point I'm trying to make here. The biggest reason I've seen for people being afraid of rejection is the thought of being embarrassed in public.

This is why telemarketers have no problem calling a thousand people a day on the phone but wouldn't approach one person in real life. This is why a lonely guy has no problem sending out hundreds of emails a day while online dating but won't approach one woman in real life.

Most of these individuals would, however, approach someone in an isolated situation where there weren't other people around. That's because the thought of trying to approach a potential client or someone of the opposite sex and getting rejected publicly can be a terrifying situation for most.

The secret to avoiding this uncomfortable situation is all in the approach. First, no matter the situation, you're interrupting someone from something they were doing prior to you approaching, so the courteous thing to do would be to excuse yourself and then apologize for interrupting them from whatever they were doing prior to your approach.

A good example of this would be to say something to the effect of "Excuse me, sir or miss, I'm so sorry to bother you, but if you don't mind, could I just get a second of your time to show you this product or service I'm offering?"

Typically, unless they're just a complete butthole, this will at least stave off an embarrassing rejection but being polite also has more benefits than that. Since you were courteous with your approach, they would usually allow you do your sales pitch. This is important because you can't sell if nobody gives you the opportunity to sell to them. All you want is a chance to sell, and this is afforded to you when you're polite and courteous with your approach.

Now I can't guarantee that this will rid yourself of 100 percent of those embarrassing approaches, because let's just be frank—there are some rude people in the world. But this would greatly diminish them.

This is also my tactic when approaching women. I usually pardon myself before introducing myself. A lot of guys are petrified of approaching women in public due to fears of being loudly rejected, but this could easily be avoided by being polite with your approach. If you approach a woman with an immature approach like "Hey, baby, what's your name?" then you get what you deserve.

Another thing to consider is that you would be surprised to know that when you're approaching individuals for sales that there really isn't anyone paying you any mind. We live in a world where everyone is consumed with social media and everything that comes with living their own lives. You may be surprised to know that nobody even notices what you're doing.

Sometimes we can be dressed a certain way, or feel a certain way, that makes us feel subconscious, and it feels like all eyes are on us, when in actuality, there isn't anyone with the slightest concern with us. More than likely it's all in your head, and nobody could give a damn about what you are doing.

Insecurities cause us to notice imperfections in ourselves which make us think that everyone else notices those same imperfections when, in actuality, if you don't bring it up, no one would even know.

Don't get me wrong; I'm well aware that you can wear or do things that could bring unwanted attention to yourself, but in those instances, if it's that outlandish, then you have to ask yourself, is the attention really unwanted?

Successful Routine

If you want to be successful, then you have to cultivate a successful routine. You can't expect to just wake up out of bed and have a successful day if it's not planned to a T. This will ensure that every second of your day is toward productivity and not a second wasted. When you don't plan your day, you also ruin the possibility of killing two birds with one stone.

For example, when I go to the gym and work out, there's a Whole Foods on my way home where I could stop by and get my groceries for the day. So I always plan to stop at the Whole Foods on my way home. This isn't my typical path home, but going in this direction doesn't make the distance home any further. It's just not my preferred path home. It's a waste of time to come home and then walk back to this Whole Foods afterward. It more productive for me stop on my way home and just take the different path as opposed to walking back to the Whole Foods.

There were times when I didn't properly plan my day and forgot to stop at Whole Foods, requiring me to make a trip to the store. This commute to the store costs me about fifteen to twenty minutes both ways, just depending on how fast I walked that particular day. That's thirty to forty minutes I could have used to be more productive, but since I didn't plan out my day, I just wasted thirty to forty minutes of it.

Trying to remember every second of your day on the fly puts you in this position, which is why I recommend using a calendar on your phone. I myself use Google Calendar, but there are others you can use as well. Back in the day, they used little date books or book schedules in which you could plan out your day on. If you prefer to do it that way, that works as well.

Plan your entire day no matter how small; it's better to write it down to prevent from forgetting. Most of these calendar apps have reminders that will alert you when you have an upcoming event or appointment approaching. You have to hold yourself accountable for sticking to your schedule you planned out. Your schedule shouldn't be something you push *ignore* on your phone when your phone alerts you of an upcoming event. Remember, you planned it for a reason.

Planning out your day doesn't mean anything if half the time an upcoming event alert goes off and you just push *ignore*. That defeats the purpose. Now, I'm aware that on occasions a prior event might go longer than previously planned, but this should be the exception and not the norm. For all intents and purposes, you should try your best to stick to the program.

Everything we do is habit forming. When you start the habit of ignoring calendar alerts, it starts to become a habit. The reason I don't want you developing this habit is because in most cases, it will be coming from a place of laziness. When you plan out your day initially, it's planned to be a productive day, but once the day arises, laziness starts to kick in, and you push the event off to another day. This starts to become a habit, and before long, you look up, and you're not accomplishing anything.

Successful individuals never put off what they can do today for tomorrow. To develop successful habits never put off what you can do today for tomorrow. When you hold yourself accountable for sticking to your schedule you ensure that your day is getting every ounce of productivity from it.

Diversify

Life is full of all kinds of challenges and curveballs. From my experience in life, it's foolish to put all your eggs in one basket. This simply means you can never expect to get rich, wealthy, or achieve financial freedom relying on one source of income.

Most millionaires and billionaires have several sources of incomes coming in. This means that if one or two sources of incomes aren't having success at the moment, they have other sources of incomes to carry the weight until the struggling sources of incomes can turn things around.

No matter your profession or business it's bound to hit a low point at some point. How can you expect to have financial freedom if you're relying on just one source of income? I think it's reasonable for anyone, with hard work of course, to obtain at least three sources of income. One active source and two that are passive.

The active source would be your profession or business you have, preferably something you have a passion for. The other two could be money you've invested from your profession or business and should be, for all intents and purposes, completely passive. That could be index funds and or real estate.

To acquire this money to invest into the stock market or real estate is going to require some delayed gratification, as I've mentioned before. From my experience, that's the hardest part to obtaining enough money to invest into the stock market and real estate. That's having the discipline to delay getting toys, like cars, jewelry, and clothing, to invest into things that don't allow you to impress your friends and family right now. Nobody cares about your stock or real estate portfolio, but a nice Rolex watch would surely turn heads.

You don't need much to invest into individual stocks, but investing in real estate does require some money down to get started, unless you're using one of those government loan programs. Mutual funds do take a lump sum to get started, as it's simply not worth a stockbroker's time to manage a fund worth a couple hundred bucks. You can buy mutual funds cheaper, but it'll be up to you to manage the account, not a stockbroker. This is why it's just easier to deal with index funds. Certain index funds do require a few thousand dollars to buy into also.

As far as getting a government mortgage loan, if it was me, I wouldn't even bother with those as they kill cash flow and inhibit you from turning a profit after paying the mortgage monthly, but that's a decision you'll have to make. Real estate and stocks won't give you the same return as starting a successful business would, but it is less of a risk. Notice that I said starting a successful business, and that's because, although starting a business can give you great returns on your investment, they are highly risky, and that risk is enhanced if you haven't done your homework or are willing to have the patience or work ethic that's required to build a successful business.

The reason stocks and real estate are less risky investments are because the housing and stock market have always rebounded, but as with opening your own business, the same holds true for stocks and real estate if you don't put the time in and do your homework.

If you go out and acquire real estate that's depreciating in value, or overpaying for property because you failed to do the necessary homework, then you run a risk of not turning a profit on your initial investment. The same can be said for buying individual stocks also. If you choose to not invest in index funds that cover the entire stock market, and balance that with bonds but fail to do your research on individual stocks, then you run the same risk of losing money on your initial investment.

You won't get wealthy overnight investing in real estate or stocks, but over time, as your property hopefully appreciates and your stocks mature with compound interest, assuming you just reinvest your dividends, then eventually, you'll be able to obtain the all-elusive financial freedom.

Debt

You hear from a lot of people today that it's better to invest than to pay off debt, if your interest rate is below a 4 or 5 percent interest rate. Their reasoning behind this is due to the fact you could make more investing in a new business, an existing business, stocks, bonds, or real estate. These are also the same individuals who think life goes in one straight linear line of progression, when in fact anyone over the age of twelve knows this is simply incorrect.

Life is full of trials and tribulations, and you're bound to hit a low point along the way. When I'm referring to hitting a low point, I'm not insinuating that you'll probably be homeless at some point, but what I am saying is that you might not be able to afford to live your current lifestyle you're living at the moment. This simply means you aren't afforded the luxury of taking your significant other out on dinner dates three nights of the week. You might not be able to afford those two international trips a year. All those are OK, as they're not necessities in life, but it's still a downgrade, nonetheless.

Now that I've gotten that out of the way, I think it's fair to say that if your financial situation is on life support, who wants the burden of a car loan around your neck? See, people who tell you to invest instead of paying off debt forget one major component to humans, and that's *stress*.

When your financial situation slows down—and it will, by the way—you will have so much less stress in your life. I can remember when my financial situation hit a low point, and I was still paying a car loan for a Chrysler 300. My stress level was at an all-time high, and when I say high, I'm referring to not sleeping well at night.

Now, when my financial situation was better, I didn't invest excess income. I did something far worse; I bought liabilities. These liabilities would come in the form of jewelry and clothing, and of course, I had to jump right back into debt with another car payment later. When my financial situation was in a better situation, I could have easily paid off my car balance, but I didn't, and now here I was with added stress in life.

Even if I had invested the money, there's a good chance I would've taken a loss because investments should always be done with long-term thinking, and you always stand to take a loss if you have to try to recoup your investment in the short term. When considering whether to pay off debt or to invest, one should always remember that we're not robots, stress is a real thing, and so is having a financial slow down at some point.

How to Develop Discipline

For all of my life up until I was at the age of thirty-four years old, I had pretty much never accomplished anything I had started. I would start off with so much dedication at the beginning, but that enthusiasm would eventually wane, and I would quit.

For some reason I had trouble maintaining the same enthusiasm for a project as did initially and couldn't, for the life of me, figure out why. It wasn't until I decided to become a certified personal trainer full time that I finally was able to finish what I started.

I then realized why I hadn't ever maintained enough discipline to finish what I started. It basically boiled down to two things. The first thing was that I simply was sick and tired of being sick and tired.

See, my earlier failures were because I hadn't got to a point in life where success was at the top of my priorities list. My earlier life consisted more of chasing women than success. Therefore, I would always lose motivation and resort back to what I did best, and that's chase women. The funny thing about that is if I had prioritized chasing success more than chasing women, I would've more than likely had a lot more success with women than I had. Chasing success makes you less available for women, which coincidently makes you more attractive, but one's primary reason for wanting to be successful can't be to attract the opposite sex. I won't say that it shouldn't even factor into the equation, because that would just be unrealistic, but it just can't be the driving factor.

The next reason I was able to finally finish a project I had started was due to the fact I was pursuing something I had a genuine passion for. See, I went to Job Corps when I was twenty years old to be an electrician, but I had about as much passion in becoming an electrician as I had in becoming a mortician. I was doing it for purely financial reasons.

There's nothing wrong with wanting to pursue something for financial reasons, in my opinion, but it should never be the main reason. Financial success should always be a byproduct of pursuing your passion in life.

In my late twenties, I actually enrolled in college to pursue a degree in IT or information technology. I have about as much passion in information technology as I do in becoming a gardener. Once again, the idea of making more money was the primary driving force behind wanting to be involved with IT.

So as you can see, it will always be hard to develop the discipline to finish what you started if the reasoning behind why you're doing it is not the right reason. You have to have a passion for what you're trying to accomplish, and you have to seriously want a change in your life.

Now to be clear, if your primary motivating factor is to make your parents proud or to attract the opposite sex, by all means use whatever you can to keep you disciplined and on track to stick to your goals. These same principles hold true for weight loss or any other goal you're hoping to accomplish. If you're having a hard time sticking to a diet, first you should make sure your diet isn't too restrictive, but in general, if your diet seems like it's impossible to stick to, maybe you haven't hit a point where you're sick and tired of being overweight.

The only way any goals happen are if you're at a point in life where failure is no longer an option.

Burnout and Change of Interest in Life

When someone embarks on a new life journey, it has a tendency to start out with lots of vigor and passion, but eventually, you start to lose steam. Now, as I've said earlier, this could very well be the result of not having a genuine passion for what you're pursuing or that you aren't fed up enough with your life as it is today.

But a couple of overlooked aspects as to why our passion for something dies down over time are that as we age our interests in life change, and we don't have enough balance in our life which ultimately leads to burnout. Burnout also happens when you start getting diminishing returns over time from your efforts.

When I was a teenager and in my early twenties, I was consumed with sports 24–7. I would watch literally every single football game that came on, and it didn't really matter who it was. I didn't care if it was a Division III football game with two teams with losing records, I'd watch it. That's how much interest I had in sports.

This obsession would wane, however, in my mid-twenties, as I then would only watch specific teams. These teams would be Michael Jordan's Wizards and the Alabama Crimson Tide. A couple years later, I also watched Lebron James's Cleveland Cavaliers. I went from watching virtually any sports game to only watching these teams, and I wouldn't even watch the Wizards or Cavaliers if Michael and Lebron weren't playing that particular game due to injury or something of that sort.

What caused this loss of enthusiasm, you ask? Well, it's simple. I simply developed a passion for something else, and that was chasing women. I had always been somewhat fascinated with pursuing women, even as a teenager, but once I reached my early twenties, it had become my new passion in life. I no longer pursued women casually in my spare time. I would now do it pretty much full time, nonstop.

Another common reason one might lose passion for an endeavor or activity is simply due to burnout. Burnout usually occurs when someone doesn't have enough balance in their life, or diminished returns become discouraging. We are not robots; we have to have some kind of socializing in our lives.

When we discover a new passion in life the excitement can lead to wanting to spend every available moment pursuing what we now desire, and that's perfectly fine, as long as you allow yourself some time to socialize. I'm all up for hard work, and to be honest, that's the only way I can legitimately see someone becoming successful, but there has to be some semblance of balance, or you run the risk of simply losing desire for what you had previously wanted to accomplish.

Whenever we start a new conquest in life, we all give ourselves some sort of timeline in our heads as to where we want to be at a certain amount of time. This also holds true when we start a new business. Pursuing your passion in life shouldn't be primarily for financial gain, but it is a component to it. Therefore, when the financial aspect isn't matching up with the amount of effort you're putting in, this could lead to burnout.

We live in a world where things cost money, so whether we want to admit it or not, money has to play a role in how we divide our time each day. You can have a passion for playing video games, but if you can't find a way to monetize that passion to support your lifestyle, you're going to have to admit to yourself at some point that you can't just sit around in your spare time and play video games if its only enhancing your life mentally.

For me, my passion in life has to enhance my life mentally and financially. I'm a responsible adult with real life bills, and if what I'm pursuing can't provide me with the financial support I need to support myself, or I simply couldn't find a way to monetize it—which does happen by the way—then maybe it's time I made that a hobby and put my energy toward something that's going to better my living situation.

Diminished returns always lead to failure, but just make sure you're giving yourself a realistic timeline as to how long it should take you to start seeing returns. Expecting to build a successful business in one year is just being unrealistic and, quite simply, ridiculous. Could you possibly do it? Of course you could, but outliers can't be your expectations. I'm coming from the aspect of it taking at least a solid three to five years.

Renting versus Buying a Home

Most individuals would say owning or buying a home is the cornerstone to achieving the American dream. While I would agree with this to a certain degree, there are a couple of scenarios where renting might actually be more beneficial than buying a home.

Let's assume you're in the process of buying a $300,000 home, and you were planning to put 20 percent down on the home to avoid paying PMI. That would mean you're spending $60,000 for the down payment, plus closing and all of the other small costs associated with purchasing a home, which would typically run you at least an additional 6 percent. This would put your grand total at a minimum of $78,000 to get the keys to the home.

Now let's assume that instead of acquiring your new home, you invested that money into starting a business or reinvested the money back into your business, if you're already a business owner. A good rate of return on your money for a successful business owner could range anywhere from 20 percent and up. For the sake of making a point, let's just say 20 percent a year was your rate of return on investment. That would mean you're making a profit of $15,600 a year after expenses.

This means that if you implemented a little self-restraint and delayed gratification, within the next five years you could get the home you initially desired and still have your cash cow business to fund your lifestyle.

Keep in mind, this is assuming that your business doesn't grow within that five years. On the other hand, you could lose your initial investment and, therefore, lose the house down payment money. This is what separates entrepreneurs from the average person: the willingness to take risks.

Now, no one I know can survive on $15,600 a year, so the business would have to be a side hustle until you can build it to something more substantial, obviously. It's these simple sacrifices that the rich are willing to do that the working poor simply fail to do.

My suggestion is if you haven't found something that truly drives you, then you're probably better off just acquiring the home due to the fact the business would more than likely fail if you're not passionate about the business you're considering starting.

Another point to consider is whether you're the type of individual who doesn't like to stay in the same location very long. I typically grow bored of the same location over a given amount of time. This could be a different state, city, or just different side of town. I just don't like to be tied down to the same location.

Now, I know what you're going to ask. Why not just rent out the house if I decide to relocate? That's a fair statement, but I'm more of the entrepreneur type than landlord. I'm a high-risk, high-reward type and would always rather invest in myself instead of rental property. Don't get me wrong; I do plan on engaging in rental property in the future, but as of right now, I'm totally invested into my Alpha Male Strategies brand, although I know the real estate game.

While it's been said that real estate has created more wealth than any other investment endeavor, I don't think it's possible to accumulate wealth faster than a successful business. I'm not suggesting you try to race to accumulate some semblance of wealth, but if you're a high-risk, high-reward type of individual, then entrepreneurship is definitely where it's at.

I do invest in index funds, however, and that's because they're completely passive and require virtually no work on my end, which means that I have more time to devote to building my business.

Analysis Paralysis

I once had a problem with procrastination, or what it's now called, *analysis paralysis*. Some might insinuate that these two terms aren't the same, and in some aspects, that might even be true. Some forms of procrastination are just flat out laziness, but when it comes to entrepreneurship, in my opinion, they're directly related.

I think it goes without saying that most adults have at some point pondered the idea of being their own boss. The reason this usually never goes any further than a pondering thought is due to all the afterthought of failure. Fear of failure, in my opinion, has to be the biggest cause of analysis paralysis.

Don't misunderstand what I'm saying. You should thoroughly analyze the steps that are needed to become your own boss, but I can tell you now, there will never be a perfect time to start your own business. You should be responsible and make sure your financial situation is stable enough to start your own business, but whether or not your finances are where they should be, the fear will always be there in the back of your mind as an entrepreneur, even when experiencing success.

In business, you could be on top one minute and filing bankruptcy the next. Courage is not about never experiencing fear; it's about conquering those fears and acting when one is experiencing fear. To be a successful entrepreneur, you have to be an individual who's basically sick and tired of working for someone. The reason I didn't include "pursuing your passion" in that last statement is due to the fact that you could technically pursue your passion working for someone else.

If being your own boss isn't the driving force behind starting your own business, then your mind could, in theory, always find reasons for you to stay an employee.

Adopting a Minimalist Lifestyle

Anybody who's familiar with my YouTube channel knows that I live in a modest apartment in New York City. Why would a man who's making four times the amount of money than when he moved into a place continue to live there once his income has increased so drastically? I'm simply implementing what I preach, which is living below your means to invest.

If you don't remember anything else from this book, just remember this: you can't build wealth trying to keep up with the Joneses. To build wealth, it means living well below your means. Let me repeat that: to build wealth you have to live *well below* your means. The key being *well below*.

At the time I'm writing this book, I make three times what I was making a year ago at this exact same time. My lifestyle, however, hasn't changed one bit, except for more free time to do whatever I want, thanks to the multiple passive income streams I've accumulated. And my expenses haven't increased one bit.

Am I saving the money? Hell no, I'm investing the excess income into my Alpha Male Strategies brand and the stock market via index funds. I'll definitely get real estate at some point in the future, but it's not in my plans right now, as building my AMS brand is first and foremost. Being a landlord isn't optimal for me right now, as being a landlord takes a lot of upfront work before it becomes passive.

I'm a firm believer that if you want to be successful or build a successful business, you have to make that your priority and give it your all. I invest in the index funds because they don't require any effort on my part to manage. If my lifestyle or expenses had increased with my income, then what would I have had to invest? Nothing. I would have just accumulated more liabilities.

This takes some serious discipline, because I would be lying if I didn't admit that sometimes, I ponder the idea of getting a new sports car like a Lamborghini, but then I would technically remain *poor*. Being poor doesn't reflect on how much money you make, but rather, it's more about your mind-set and how much money you keep.

There are a lot of rich poor people in the world. A rich poor person is an individual that makes a lot of money but has very little savings or investments due to an extravagant lifestyle. This is the type of individual who makes a million dollars a month, but it still isn't enough due to their expenses. This makes them poor due to the fact they couldn't handle any life emergencies that are bound to arise eventually. They're one slip and fall away from losing everything.

I know this because I've been there before in my life. There have been two occasions in my life where I had to move in with family members after losing my job because I had virtually no savings. When I worked the job, I didn't feel poor because I had a check every Friday that I could depend on. But you're flirting with disaster if you don't have a solid savings of at least three months of living expenses.

If you have one individual who makes forty grand a year, but has a solid six months of living expenses saved, and another individual who makes six million a year, but doesn't have any safety net money saved, then the individual who makes forty grand is technically better off financially.

Another aspect with being poor is the mentality. If you gave a poor man—and by poor, I'm referring to his mind-set not his financial situation—$10,000, he would probably go buy some clothing, a car, and some jewelry if he had anything left. If a rich man—and by rich, I'm referring to the mind-set, not his financial situation—was given $10,000, he would figure out the best way to flip that money so he could later buy the liabilities and still have the $10,000 creating him income.

That's the biggest difference I see between poor and rich people—the mind-set. To live a minimalist lifestyle, you have to cut out all unnecessary expenses. This requires eating at home more than you eat out. This requires you to buy non-trendy clothing. Trendy clothing is the kind of clothing that is in style one season and out of style the next season. It requires you to keep your ten-year-old car a few more years, even though you're tired of it. This means you're living at your current location a little while longer to invest, even though that downtown spot looks so much sexier.

If you want to lose your poor mind-set, it first starts with knowing that sacrifices have to be made in order to achieve your desired outcome.

How to Build Your Social Media

There was once a time where it was virtually impossible to get your products and services in front of consumers without a substantial financial backing. That doesn't hold true these days.

Anyone can place their products in front of potential consumers, thanks to a thing called social media. What was once used to keep up with old classmates and drifting friendships is now used by the business-minded as free product placement. Thanks to social media, there's no need to beg a publishing company to take you on as a client to promote your book, or a record company to give you a contract as an artist.

These things were needed back in the day because without the financial backing of a publishing company or a record contract from a big record label, you simply couldn't get your product in front of consumers unless you had some serious cash flow or investors.

Having a big YouTube following myself, I get companies wanting me to endorse their products all the time, but I always decline due to the fact that they're always products I've never used, and therefore, ethically, I couldn't endorse their product. That's the complete definition of a sellout in my opinion.

I do wonder however, why don't they just do what I did and build their own social media following? The answer is quite simple: building a social media following is hard, tedious work, and most individuals are just looking for a shortcut.

It would be like me writing this book, without having a social media following, and then contacting a social media influencer to promote my book to their following with me giving them a discount code to use so they can make money. This only benefits the product owner, however, since most individuals won't even use the discount code, as it's usually so minuscule that it isn't even worth using. This is another reason why I don't endorse others' products, because I know it usually only benefits them.

Building a solid social media following can take a few years, but there are occasions it can happen a little faster. It took me only a year to accumulate over one hundred thousand subscribers on YouTube. You can accumulate as many subscribers as you want, but if you don't have a product to sell, then it's useless.

To build a following, it helps to have a personality, but that isn't a necessity. Having camera presence usually helps, however, as it helps maintain the followers' attention without them growing tired of you. We live in a society today where millennials have such a short attention spans, and even some older individuals have this also.

If you're planning on building a solid social media following, you have to be consistent with your uploads. You don't have to upload every single day, but it can't be every couple of months either. At least once a week is a good rule to go by, with anything more being a bonus.

You can overdo the uploads however as you can burn out your followers with content. It really just boils down to what niche you're involved with. A fitness video or picture upload every day might be acceptable, while a vlog about your life might be overkill.

I've been critical of men in the past using social media to just admire women, while women use it to make money. Once upon a time, women only used social media for free attention and validation, but not any longer. There are some women who still use social media for validation, but an increasing majority of women use it to sell some sort of product.

Of course, you have some women who use it for neither, as they don't post any provocative pictures to receive attention and validation. They use it for the simple purpose of keeping up with friends and family. I'm hoping that more men start seeing the potential in social media from a business aspect and use it to promote their products and services.

When you're building a social media following, you're basically building a customer base at the same time.

Victim Mentality

I was raised to basically accept being poor as a way of living, and there was nothing I could do about it. I think it's fair to say that it's a very large segment of the public who are raised with these same beliefs. I was raised to believe that everyone rich inherited their money, was an athlete, entertainer or lottery winner.

Sure, in school they tell you that you can become anything you want if you apply yourself, but then they would turn around and teach us how to become employees. Nowhere in school do they teach you how to invest your money, or the difference between liabilities and assets. I don't ever remember being taught in school about the difference between passive income and active income.

I was however in high school taught how to prepare a resume. If you want to be successful and acquire wealth, you have to rid yourself of your victim mentality. There is no *they*. *The Man* is not holding you down. You are holding yourself down, or rather, your mind-set is holding you down.

There are rich people represented by every race, gender, and sexual preference. The overwhelming majority of wealthy individuals are self-made, and that's a fact, not an opinion. It's easier to make excuses rather than put the work into accomplishing what you're trying to accomplish.

Let me say this as emphatically as I can say it: *you can accumulate as much wealth as you want if you're willing to put the work in.* It's just that simple, but that victim mind-set has to go.

At the time of writing this book, it was approximately five and half years ago when my life changed forever, and no, I didn't win the lottery. I rid myself of the previous victim mentality that had held me back my entire life. I remember my first day working at the gym that I had just hired me, and all I could think was, it's up to me now to change my life forever. I was in a position to get sales and make well over a $100,000 a year, depending on how much work I was willing to put in.

Donald Trump wasn't going to stop me. The Rockefellers weren't there to hold me back. There weren't any society elites to hold me down. My success was based entirely on how many sales I could generate any given day.

Those sales numbers were mainly based on how many hours I was willing to spend on the floor and how many approaches I would do in those hours I was on the floor. Most trainers would quit because they had the victim mentality. They were more concerned with why the managers weren't sending them clients instead of taking responsibility and building their own clientele base.

See, this is what's wrong with the victim mentality. You either want the higher-ups to help you, or you blame them for your shortcomings.

Let me lay out the blueprint for success. There isn't a single human on earth that can stop you from accomplishing your goals. Invest in yourself first by getting a skill or education, preferably in something you have a passion for, but not a necessity if you haven't figured out your purpose in life yet. Bust your ass for a couple of years in the work force living below your means so you can save your money. After you've accumulated a significant amount of money, all the while enhancing your skills in the workforce, you can hopefully start your own business if you're the ambitious type.

If you're not the entrepreneur type, you can still buy money-making assets like real estate or stocks to supplement your income. If you're the entrepreneur type, you bust your behind for a few years to build your business before you invest in other moneymaking assets like real estate and stocks. The reasoning behind this is if you want to grow your business efficiently, it'll require you to reinvest your profits back into the business for several years. Once your business is at a point that you're financially comfortable with, it's time to invest into other money-making assets.

I just laid out a few sentences that basically give you the blueprint for acquiring wealth, and there's nothing The Man can do about it if you're willing to put the work in.

Pros and Cons to Entrepreneurship

There was a saying by one of my favorite bodybuilders of all time, Ronnie Coleman, that has always stuck with me throughout my life. He would say before and after performing one of his many heavy set of lifts in the gym, "Everybody wants to be a bodybuilder, but don't nobody want to lift no heavy-ass weight." This correlates directly with entrepreneurship because everybody wants to be an entrepreneur, but nobody wants to put the work and sacrifices in to build a business.

There are several pros to being an entrepreneur, but there are some cons as well. The pros are that you're your own boss and technically don't have to answer to anyone. I say technically because I guess it can be said that you have to answer to your customers to some degree. If you don't keep your customers happy, then you won't have a business.

You're free to make the hours you want to work, there's no boss telling you the hours he wants you to work. There's also a level of pride you have when you're your own boss. Selling your time for money is a thing of the past when you're an entrepreneur. Maybe you have to sell your time for money initially at the beginning stages of your business, but once you've built the business, you can simply hire employees to work the business for you.

I think a big aspect to entrepreneurship that's overlooked is the tax breaks that business owners are given. The government wants business owners to succeed because they're the job creators that drive the economy. Therefore, the government does everything it possibly can by means of tax breaks to help business owners succeed. If you're unaware or unfamiliar with these tax breaks, be sure to check with a certified tax accountant.

As great as all this sounds, it's not all champagne and roses as an entrepreneur. One of the cons you'll encounter as an entrepreneur are long workdays. One of the biggest misconceptions that persists is that when you're an entrepreneur, you hardly work. Most of the working middle class think business owners play golf and travel in first class every day. This is true of some wealthy individuals, though even most of those had to work their butts off to get their life to the point where they can actually do that.

But the overwhelming majority of entrepreneurs in this country are not even wealthy, not to mention having their business to the point where they don't even work. The average successful entrepreneur works a whole lot more than the average working person. Sixty-plus hour workweeks are not uncommon, so if you have ambitions of being a successful entrepreneur, be prepared to give up a lot of your social life.

Once you've gotten your business to the point where you can actually hire employees, you now have the responsibility of other families depending on you to keep food on the table and a roof over their heads. A slip in business not only affects you but other families as well. That's a lot of pressure to say the least.

As a business owner you may be forced to make very tough decisions at times. These tough decisions can come in the form of laying employees off, if that's what's best for the bottom line. You're running a business not a charity foundation, and the bottom line has to always play a major part in your decisions.

Some business owners say to always do what's best for the bottom line, and while I do agree with that assertion to some degree, we're not robots, and emotions do come into play occasionally, unless you're a heartless butthole.

In my opinion, there's no faster way to accumulate wealth than being an entrepreneur, but it's also perhaps the riskiest investment you can make, as most businesses fail the first year. Let's assume you took your life savings of $40,000 and decided to start a business, as opposed to investing it into more reliable investments like real estate or the stock market. If your business fails for whatever reason, you couldn't help but think to yourself, "If I had just invested that $40,000 into index funds, my money could've been earning an average return of 6–10 percent annually."

On the other hand, if your business is successful, it's not unheard of to get over a 100 percent return on investment the first year, if executed perfectly. The age-old adage holds true here, the higher the risk, the higher the rewards.

Pros and Cons to the Stock Market

The stock market is one of the best ways that I know of to create absolutely passive income. One of the pros to investing into the stock market is that it requires virtually no effort on your part to create passive income, if you're investing in index funds that cover the entire stock market, of course.

If you're buying individual stocks, then that's a different story. Like I said before, buying individual stocks is a lot riskier, but it can be more rewarding if done correctly. Most streams of passive income require a lot of work up front to get it to a point to where's it relatively passive.

Real estate and entrepreneurship are never 100 percent passive. The real estate can be, if you decide to hire a property manager.

One detriment to investing into the stock market is that you have absolutely no control. You have control on whether to invest your money into a company, but that investment gives you no say-so as to how the company conducts its business.

When you make other investments, you have control as to how that money is delegated. If you have a partner or partners, you have to come to some sort of agreement as to how the business is run and money delegated. If you have business partners, but your stake in the company is so minuscule that you really don't have a say, they'll at least take your opinions into considerations.

When you invest into companies in the stock market, they have their own board of trustees, and your opinions don't matter, relatively speaking. They do, however, listen to consumers' product complaints, but that's about it. When you invest your money into other things like a business or real estate, you have the peace of mind knowing that your success depends for the most part on your decision-making and the amount of effort you put forth.

If things don't go according to plan, you have the peace of mind knowing you have no one else to blame but yourself. Another downside to investing into the stock market is that it has to be a completely long-term strategy, because stocks go up and down daily, and if a major emergency was to arise, and you absolutely needed money, you could take out a loan against the money you have invested into the stock market, but that would mean you're in debt.

I would rather sell my stocks than go back into debt again. Either one is not a desirable decision as your stocks could be down at that very moment, meaning you've probably lost a considerable amount of money.

You should have a proper savings for emergencies anyway, but sometimes, even that may not be enough. I don't reference cryptocurrency in this book, and that's because I don't believe in it. I think it's a fad, but I could be wrong. I prefer investing into things that have a proven track record over an extended period of time.

Who knows, maybe twenty years from now, with a consistent track record of growth over that period of time, I'll be more inclined to invest into cryptocurrency. I make smart investments with my money, not emotional decisions based on a couple years of data. When you take this approach with investing, you're less likely to encounter a loss, as opposed to just jumping on a whim.

As I've mentioned before, however, crypto can be referred to as one of those high-risk, high-rewards type investments. The highest risk I'm willing to bet on any investment is in myself by way of business. See, a business is high-risk and high-reward, but I don't look at it quite that way, as I believe I can accomplish anything I put my mind to. When you invest into crypto or stocks, you have absolutely no control over those markets and are thus vulnerable to whatever the market gives you.

Pros and Cons to Real Estate

I think we all know or have heard of an unruly tenant. Real estate can be one of the best investments you can make, but if you were to ever encounter an unruly tenant, it could literally turn into a nightmare. You could just flip real estate and not have to deal with tenants altogether, but if you go the landlord route, be prepared to encounter bad tenants from time to time.

Flipping houses is when you buy a property and put money into it to sell for a profit. Another downside to being a landlord is trying to keep the property rented out. There could be months where you have no tenant paying you money, killing cash flow. It's an even bigger problem if you're using leverage and have a mortgage on the property. This could cause financial hardship if you're not prepared for this type of situation.

A lot of landlords anticipate the property always being rented out and never take into account the financial impact on them it would have if the property went vacant for a few months.

This is the biggest detriment to using leverage to create wealth. It works well until it doesn't. Leverage is when you use debt to make money. Leverage is used heavily in real estate.

Let's not forget the tenant that destroys your property. Some security deposits can't make up for the damage some tenants cause to properties. If you decide to do real estate and go the route of landlord, you'll need to have done your due diligence when checking prospective tenant's credit and background.

One important aspect to being a landlord that is sometimes overlooked is checking with the potential tenant's previous landlord to find out what type of tenant they were previously. Most bad tenants didn't become bad tenants overnight. There's usually a history there. If you're going to invest your hard-earned money into a rental property, I think it would be smart on your part to leave no stone unturned when finding a suitable tenant.

There's a saying in real estate that it's not *if* you'll end up in court, but *when*. What this is saying is that at some point, you can expect to have to evict a tenant, or something of that nature that eventually puts you in a courtroom. Just giving you the heads up.

Real estate has many benefits, as you may well know, including being one of the most reliable ways to create wealth. It doesn't create wealth as fast as a successful business, but it's much more reliable and steadier.

Once you've gone through the process of renovating the property, if need be, and finding suitable tenants for the property, it can become mostly passive income aside from the occasional property maintenance. Even that can be avoided, if you were to hire a property manager to maintain the residence. Most property management companies do require a certain amount of properties to manage, however.

I recommend applying for a traditional mortgage, which is typically a thirty-year fixed mortgage. This means your interest rate is fixed and can't be changed. The reason I recommend the thirty-year mortgage over the fifteen-year mortgage is that it allows more flexibility in the event of future financial difficulties.

One should strive to pay off the mortgage as soon as possible, however, to avoid paying as much interest as possible, but the thirty-year mortgage offers a little less stress in the event of unforeseen hard times. This doesn't mean you go out and get the biggest house a bank approves you for. This will inevitably leave you as what is commonly known as house-poor.

Being house-poor means that an individual can't save or invest money due to their home eating away at any and all disposable income. This is usually the case if your intentions for the home are for you, as opposed to renting it out, but individuals have been guilty of this with rental properties as well. What's the point in owning a home if you can't even live your life?

This is of even more importance if you're planning on using the property as rental property because you can't always find tenants, and quite frankly, you should expect the rental property to be vacant at times. This means that you're on the hook for paying the mortgage, despite having your own living situation to account for.

A bank might approve you for something because they don't take into account a financial slowdown. They typically just look at your previous two or three years of financial statements and approve you on that without ever taking into account a financial downfall.

Another great benefit to real estate is the opportunity to house hack. House hacking is when you purchase a multi-family home and let your tenant or tenants pay down the mortgage while you live there virtually free, allowing you to use your income for other investments.

My biggest concern, as far as real estate goes, is if you're unable to put down the 20 percent needed to avoid PMI. If you can't afford to put down the 20 percent needed to avoid the mortgage insurance, then it stands to reason that you don't have enough of savings to carry you in the event of an extended property vacancy. This will inevitably cause you to fall into a desperate situation. This is what causes landlords to rent out a property to a tenant with a less than stellar credit record.

I think real estate is a good investment if you can buy the property outright or, at the very minimum, put down the 20 percent needed to avoid the mortgage insurance. If you can't afford the property outright and have to take on a mortgage payment, then you should make sure you have enough of a savings to cover the newly acquired mortgage as well as all of your other monthly living expenses for no less than six months. This will prevent you from falling into a desperate situation, causing you to rent your property out to very risky tenants.

How to Get Rich

I think it's a pretty safe statement to assume that pretty much anyone living today would enjoy the opportunity to become rich. Even if their motivation to become rich wasn't to acquire material assets or traveling the world, but rather to help the poor and or sick. Regardless of the reason we would want to become rich, the same denominator remains the same: it takes money. Everyone wants to become rich, but unfortunately not everyone knows what it takes to get rich.

Now, everyone has a different barometer of what exactly rich is to them, so for the sake of making a point, I'll use my own barometer of what's rich to me. Being rich to me means you can afford an extravagant lifestyle. An extravagant lifestyle means that you can afford luxuries the middle class simply can't afford. These are the hated and envied 1 percent.

At the time of writing this, the 1 percent was making, on average, $421,926 a year. Now that's my definition of rich, but I'm well aware that most people would disagree with that assertion, and that's fine.

A doctor or a lawyer who works eighty to 100 hours a week to make over a $500,000 a year is considered rich. This is why I'm not simply motivated to be rich. The reason I make a bold statement like that is because they aren't living a fulfilling lifestyle unless it's a true passion of theirs. There are some doctors and lawyers who very well may enjoy their profession, and if they do, kudos to them, but I think it would be a fair statement to say that most doctors and lawyers chose their prospective professions for monetary gains.

And there's nothing wrong with that, because some people who go through their entire life and never discover their purpose in life, the same way a lot of people go through their entire life and never get an opportunity to experience true love. If you're one of the lucky ones to discover your purpose in life or experience unconditional love, consider yourself lucky because there are a lot of individuals who can't say the same.

To me, being rich means you have the money but not the lifestyle I desire. Another thing to consider is that if you're a doctor or lawyer, and you stop practicing your profession, you won't be able to maintain your lifestyle.

So what's the solution to becoming rich if trading time for money doesn't make you rich indefinitely? The answer is to create a program, product, book, self-run business, or course, or build enough tangible and non-tangible assets, like real estate or stocks, that make you passive income that can maintain your current lifestyle.

Of course, you always have the entertainment industry, but I'm keeping this on a practical basis, as most individuals won't have the talent to make it in the entertainment industry.

Other than acquiring tangible and nontangible assets that appreciate over time, the answer is to help people, but you don't want to help people one at a time. You want to help people with your knowledge on a particular subject, but not on an individual basis. You want to help them on a large scale. You can do this by creating a course, a self-help or improvement book, etc.

If you're a personal trainer, you'll never get rich training clients individually because there are only so many hours in a day. On the other hand, let's say you created an app or diet plan for your followers to purchase 24–7 online, and now you're talking.

This goes back to what I said previously in the book of why you want to build a social media following. If you're a police officer, you'll never get rich being a police officer, but let's say you wrote a book on how to better prevent yourself from becoming a victim of crime—after building a social media following, of course—and riches could soon follow.

No matter what course, book, or program you created, the key is to somehow help people. In doing so, it's so fulfilling because not only are you making monetary gains, but you're actually adding to people's lives. It's a great feeling when people email you informing you of how much value you've added to their lives.

Of course, people will pay for entertainment also, so if you can create a product that entertains people, you're still enhancing their life. You're allowing them, for a few minutes out the day, to escape their reality and be happily entertained.

This form of entertainment can come in many fashions. It could be a game, puzzle, app, music, club, book etc. To create something that's entertaining and original, you have to have a very creative side. But if that's you, then go ahead because the entertainment industry is one of the most lucrative industries there is.

You can also become rich by way of tangible and nontangible assets that appreciate. This usually requires time to get your investment portfolio to create enough passive income to sustain your lifestyle without you actively working again, but it can be done—faster for some than others. It really just depends on how much and fast you can invest your money. Like I've said before, this issue is going to come down to two primary factors, having a high-paying skill and keeping expenses to a minimum.

Rich versus Wealthy

Most of society doesn't know that there are levels to living an affluent lifestyle. You have two classes when it comes to an affluent lifestyle. There are rich people and wealthy people. Being classified rich in America is when you make over $421,926 a year. Although this is a nice income, it doesn't take into account the number of hours you had to work to make that amount of income.

There are some doctors, lawyers and other professions that make this type of income but most of them require working well past the accustomed forty-hour workweek.

In my opinion, just being rich isn't that desirable. Being wealthy is much more desirable to me because being wealthy, in my opinion, means you not only make a rich person's salary, but you make your hefty income passively. Being wealthy, in my opinion, means you've not only achieved the elusive financial freedom, but you can afford to live a luxurious lifestyle, all the while earning your money mostly passively. This means you actually have time to enjoy your money.

I've trained doctors and lawyers who worked a hundred hours a week. You don't need to be wealthy to achieve financial freedom, but being wealthy means you're able to live a luxurious lifestyle without actively working much. Wealth is also something that's generational and the amount of passive income is so enormous that it's passed down for many generations.

Take me writing these books for instance. If my books and other passive investments I have ever get to a point that they are generating over $421,926 a year, then that would make me wealthy in my book. I don't need to make $421,926 a year, however, to achieve financial freedom.

The average person thinks rich and wealthy people don't enjoy luxuries in life, and this is simply not true. Mainstream media wants you to believe that wealthy individuals only buy assets and eat cat food to save on expenses. This couldn't be the farthest thing from the truth.

Rich people wear things that cost a lot of money but aren't exactly flashy. In other words, that polo shirt your boss wears may look like it cost $20, but in reality, it cost $400. They do, however, employ a little delayed gratification and purchase luxury items once their investments start paying off. I went to the Ralph Lauren shopping store on the upper east side of Manhattan, and they had cashmere polo shirts in there that cost over $900. What was odd to me was that, other than the fabric, it looked no different than the average polo shirt. The cashier told me he couldn't keep the cashmere shirts in the store.

The reason rich people buy these shirts kills two birds with one stone. The cashmere allows for the greatest comfort, and their friends know the quality of the shirt even though you may not.

See, that's the thing. There are so many luxury brands out there, other than Gucci and Louis Vuitton. If you go on Instagram, you will see there's no shortage of rich people wearing expensive luxury brands. The only difference between you and them is that they're buying their luxuries from appreciating assets and passive income, while you are acquiring yours from active income.

There are some very wealthy individuals who you never see doing this, however, but I'm willing to bet almost anything that they're very self-conscious of their public image and choose to enjoy their luxuries in private away from the public. This might not be clothing or jewelry, but you would have a hard time convincing me that they don't have some sort of expensive vice or habit they engage in privately. Maybe it's not expensive by their standards but would seem extravagant to the average individual.

This notion of rich and wealthy people not trying to keep up with appearances is ridiculous. Why else do you think a family of four would buy a home with twenty bedrooms? I'm well aware of the handful of frugal billionaires who live far below their means, but that is the minority and not the majority. Another reason wealthy people live far below their means is that they have no choice for the most part. If you're wealthy and have multiple streams of passive income, it's virtually impossible to spend that type of money unless you were deliberately trying to be wasteful.

Inflation

I was raised to save my money for a rainy day. This is how most of the poor in this country are raised—to save and to buy liabilities, to be exact. The saving money part isn't exactly the worst thing in the world, but I don't think the people who make this assertion are aware of a thing called inflation.

Inflation is when your money loses value over time. To put it in simpler terms, if you have $500 in your bank account right now, that $500 has a lot less purchasing power five years from now. It's actually losing value on a daily basis. It's probably not enough to register, but over time this small amount adds up enormously.

Currently inflation hovers around the 2 percent per year mark. This means that if you have $100 in your pocket, by the end of the year, it's worth only $98. Over five years, it would only be worth somewhere around $90. I know a lot of people are petrified to invest their money, but you should be petrified of your money losing value on a daily basis.

We all have different levels of risk tolerance, but if investing frightens you that much, I would invest in things like CDs that aren't risky at all. CDs are certificates of deposit that you get through a bank. Basically, you're loaning the bank money. The bank then takes the money and usually loans it out. ROI varies, but it really depends on the length of time of the CD. In other words, a five-year CD typically pays more than a one-year CD, depending on which bank you use.

I've seen CDs pay as much as 3.5 percent, which, coincidentally is higher than inflation. So, if you're petrified of investing in the stock market, or don't want to deal with the headache associated with being a landlord, then do yourself a favor and at least invest in CDs. They aren't the best investment, but they're better than the average savings account rates. At the very least, your money won't be depreciating. The only caveat is your money is tied up and can't be touched unless you want to pay a penalty. This penalty can come in the way of forfeiting several months of interest, which basically kills the reason you invested in the first place.

A good way to avoid this is by not investing all of your money and keeping at least six months' worth of expenses liquid at all times. This six months' worth of liquid assets does not have to lose value if you keep it in an online bank like Ally or American Express, which offer interest rates slightly higher than inflation.

How to Deal with Stress

If you have ambitions to become an entrepreneur, landlord, or to invest into stocks, there's always going to be some type of stress associated with it. One of the primary reasons the average person doesn't want to deal with entrepreneurship is the stress they know that undoubtedly comes associated with it.

There's typically less stress with just working a typical nine-to-five than starting your own business. Don't even get me started with having bad tenants who don't pay on time month after month. Oh, did I mention watching a stock you've invested heavily into tank day after day while you try to stay the course?

Once you've achieved financial freedom, it's a great feeling, but very few talk about the stress associated with achieving it. No matter how rich or how poor you are, stress is a part your life. How you deal with that stress varies from person to person.

There are two ways to primarily deal with stress, that's proactively and reactively. It's obviously better to deal with stress proactively, which helps prevent stress tremendously, but there's no 100 percent sure way to rid your life of stress to my knowledge. Although there's no surefire way to rid your life of stress, exercising, diet, meditating, ridding your life of toxic individuals, living within your means, and regular massages, if one can afford them, go a very long way toward reducing stress and may kill it altogether in some cases.

Exercising helps by eliminating that built up tension you have. I should emphasize that moderate to intense training does this, not sitting on the exercise bike with your heart rate hovering around the ninety beats per minute range. While something is better than nothing, you want to engage in activities that get the heart rate up and cause you to sweat. Sweating allows the body to purify itself by releasing toxins through your sweat. Moderate to intense exercising also helps with blood flow and keeping blood pressure in check.

We invite a lot of stress when we invite negative individuals into our lives. This could be by the means of family members, friends, co-workers etc. Just think to yourself how peaceful your life would be if you rid yourself of toxic individuals. They rarely have anything positive to say about anyone or anything. Gossip and negativity are their life's calling which, in turn, leaves you paranoid if they're gossiping about you when you're not around.

I think the biggest cause of stress I've encountered in my lifetime was from living beyond my means. When you live beyond your means every month, around bill time can become very stressful to say the least. Every time you pay the bills, you breathe a sigh of relief only to know you were going to have to encounter the exact same situation the very next month. This type of stress is a stress that rides with you 24–7 and never really goes away through the month.

Meditating is another great way to relieve stress. Meditating doesn't mean you have to become a Buddhist. It simply means you regularly engage in activities that relax the body and mind. Yoga, to me, is a meditating method that not only improves flexibility and stability, but also mental capacity. Yoga was once frowned upon by most men who followed the body building lifestyle, as it didn't look like the most masculine thing to engage in, but that no longer holds true as more and more men are partaking in the activity.

One overlooked way to relieve stress is receiving regular massages, particularly in the trapezius areas. It's a commonly known fact that stress is related to neck muscle stiffness. Massages relieve muscle tension, which in turn relieves the toxins these muscle knots have accumulated. Ridding the body of these toxins by way of massages and sweating are pivotal for stress relief. I'm aware of the fact that not every individual is capable of affording a massage on a regular basis, but you can also release tight muscles by way of foam rollers and trigger point balls if massages are a little outside of your budget.

The things I've laid out to try should be done preferably proactively to greatly diminish the possibility of being in a stressful state, but if you haven't been engaging in these activities you can give them a try and they should bring down your stress levels tremendously.

Depression

If you're the type of individual who gets tunnel vision when you're trying to accomplish something, then falling into a bout of depression isn't all that uncommon. When you have tunnel vision you can become isolated, resulting in a small bout of depression. Most times, this could be temporary and fixed with just living a more balanced social lifestyle. Sometimes it requires seeking medical help.

When I'm focused on something it can literally take over my life. Fortunately for me, I've never had to seek medical help. I just start to feel too isolated and then incorporate more of a social life.

Millions of people suffer from depression at some point in their life. Depression is something that should be taken very seriously. A simple pep talk with yourself isn't going to cure the symptoms of depression.

As with stress, there are things you can do proactively to help you from entering a state of depression. Exercising, proper diet, finding your purpose in life, and a proper work-life balance.

Entrepreneurs or individuals with strong work ethics can find themselves in a situation where they don't have enough of a social life, causing them to fall into a state of depression. I've had this issue with building my AMS brand, where I literally would work 100-hour workweeks from home with very little social interaction. This is simply not healthy mentally.

Maybe you can get away with it for a short period of time, but if done continuously, you will likely find yourself in a state of depression. We're social creatures, and when we limit ourselves from human contact for extended periods of time, not only do we lose social skills from lack of human interaction, but it's very unhealthy from a mental standpoint. More human interaction may limit your chances of falling into a state of depression, but it won't limit it altogether.

I know this simply from the fact that there are many social individuals who suffer from depression. If fixing depression was as simple as more interaction, then there would be no social individuals suffering from depression.

Finding one's purpose in life does wonders when dealing with depression. When you're working a job for either to twelve hours a day, and you absolutely hate what you're doing for a living, that's enough to cause depression in almost anyone. We have to work for a living, so this typically means you spend a third of your workday doing something you hate.

You can't let fear of failure have you doing a job you hate for the rest of your working life. Find out what you have a passion for in life and go after it. As with having a better work-life balance, finding your purpose won't 100 percent limit the chances of falling into a state of depression. I think we all know plenty of rich and famous people who seemed happy, only to commit suicide.

I know some of you may say, "Well, maybe they hadn't found their true passion in life," and I guess that could be true. But I would counter that assessment with there's no way you could get to that type of success in life without being very passionate about what you're doing. Even with a lot of natural talent it takes a lot of hard work and dedication to become successful.

Diet and exercise help tremendously because they keep our hormones balanced—especially diet. I won't get into what this diet should consist of, as people these days take diets more seriously than religion. You have vegans, vegetarians, intermittent fasting, organic diets, etc. Any diet that I would suggest outside of what someone follows is surely to get me the death sentence.

I recommend anyone who thinks they might be suffering from depression in the slightest way to go see a doctor. When you suffer from a chemical or hormonal imbalance, a doctor may be the only person who can help you. Maybe a simple lifestyle adjustment is all you need, but this is something a doctor can recommend.

Thinking that a simple lifestyle adjustment will do the trick entirely is false, simply on the premise of insinuating that there aren't any healthy individuals who are depressed. While I don't know any myself, I think it's safe to say that somewhere in the world, there is an individual who lives a very organic lifestyle with a very rigorous workout regimen who is still depressed.

While the things I've laid out should help anyone reduce the chances of falling into a state of a depression, I still don't think there's a foolproof method that prevents depression.

Pass Your Mind-Set Down

I was raised poor, but what was even worse, I was raised with a poor mind-set. A poor mind-set is when you're basically taught to accept the mediocrity of working a lackluster nine-to-five. There's nothing wrong with working a nine-to-five as long as it's fulfilling to you, but if you're working a job you hate because you've been conditioned to think this is the only thing life has to offer, then that's a different story.

When you build wealth, not only is the wealth passed down, but the mind-set to build that wealth is also typically passed down. There are occasions where relatives of wealthy individuals obviously didn't inherit the wealthy individual's mind-set because they spend their time just blowing money instead of creating more wealth. But I would say that this is the minority and not the majority.

The ones who don't inherit the mind-set are usually from a situation where the wealthy individual who passed didn't give the relatives any guidelines as to what they expected from them.

Bill Gates has already stated he's donating most of his money to charity and not passing it down to his kids, which will inevitably cause them to create their own wealth, and this is what I plan on doing with my relatives or children, if I ever decide to have any in the future. Bill Gates has said that he'll pay for their education and leave them something, but he wants them to create their own path in the world. The name Gates alone should do wonders for opening doors for them.

What I do plan on passing down however is this new entrepreneurial mind-set I've developed in my late thirties. Creating wealth is as simple as adopting a delayed gratification lifestyle to invest your money, plain and simple. No Albert Einstein or Thomas Edison formulas needed—it's that simple.

You can go with the high-risk route of creating a business, or you can go with the more conventional, slower but safer route of buying real estate or investing in the stock market. You can also go the more conventional path to success of creating a thriving business, and then investing into slower passive investments like real estate and stocks.

With me developing this mind-set now, I hope my family is set for generations to come. If I do decide to have kids in the future, I plan to teach them this mind-set and let them know that they can create their own wealth. It's nice to pass money down, but the best thing you could ever do is pass down the mind-set needed to create that wealth.

Reward System

Delayed gratification is a must if you ever hope to obtain any semblance of wealth, but too much of anything is never good. This holds true with rewarding yourself from time to time—whether it be sacrificing delicious fattening foods, to losing weight or sacrificing material items and vacationing, to invest your money to create more income.

While sacrificing is a necessary and almost mandatory ingredient to accomplish almost anything you're trying to accomplish, you have to reward yourself from time to time to keep yourself motivated and from burning out.

Depriving yourself of these rewards shows a short-term mind-set, as you think of creating wealth as a sprint rather than a marathon. When you treat accomplishments like a sprint rather than a marathon, a burnout is likely.

Being a personal trainer for many years myself, I saw this with many newcomers to the gym. They would start the new year out with these two-hour marathon sessions while probably eating minimal calories. As you may have expected, they would eventually just quit the gym altogether. The human body and mind don't work that way. We have to release those happy endorphins in our minds from time to time.

This doesn't mean you treat yourself every payday with a new outfit or shoes, however. I recommend rewarding yourself whenever you've accomplished a major milestone in your new endeavor. For example, I reward myself with a small spending spree whenever I release a new book. This doesn't mean I empty my bank account, but I do, however, get whatever I want within reason. That "within reason" is going to depend on your income. What's within reason to one individual might be totally different to another individual. With my diet, I reward myself much more often than I do with my business because I've seen for myself cheating on my diet actually helps me lose weight.

I don't recommend applying this same principle to your financial situation, however, as you won't accumulate any money to invest. Usually, once or twice a year should suffice. Don't worry about losing ground with your savings, as I've discovered it actually kept me more motivated in the long term.

Rules to Buying Luxury Items

Treating yourself from time to time is a very good idea, in my opinion, but there are rules to buying luxury items that everyone looking to get the most for their money should follow.

First and foremost, treating yourself should not be to impress others, although it does cross our minds, sadly. Let's face it, one of the biggest joys to buying ourselves material items is to make others jealous to some degree. Then after making others jealous we're puzzled as to why others are hating on us, when in actuality, that's exactly what we wanted. In that aspect, we're a walking contradiction.

Whatever your motivation for buying nice things, it does make us feel better about ourselves. If nothing else, it serves as a scorecard of sorts to show us the fruits of our labor. Buying cars is like the American pastime when it comes to splurging on ourselves. What better reminder to everyone around you of how good you're doing in life, or how much debt you're in to people who know you couldn't afford to buy that car cash?

When buying a car, while brand does come into play, dependability should play a bigger role than brand. You don't need the new Mercedes Maybach to get from point A to point B. On the other hand, you don't want a $500 car that has to be put in the repair shop every other week, either.

So what's the compromise? Well, I don't want to associate a price to it, because everyone's financial situation is different, but it should be at least four years old, as most cars lose most of their depreciation within the first four years.

Purchasing another car should be done only if you need a better car for dependability, and you can afford it in cash. If you're looking to create wealth, you'll never accomplish it with the mind-set of impressing others. Going into debt shouldn't even be an option after you've adopted your new mind-set.

Jewelry is another thing we splurge on when we have disposable income. Some people actually purchase jewelry with indispensable income and go into debt to purchase it, which is the opposite of wealth accumulation. If you want to reward or treat yourself with jewelry, there are a lot of items that actually appreciate. A lot of high-end watches, like Rolexes in some instances, actually appreciate.

Appreciation aside, I think it's very cool to be able to wear a $30,000 Rolex for ten years, and for whatever reason, if or when I decide to sell it, I can expect to at least get my money back if I've kept it in good condition. This doesn't hold true for broken-down watches that have the diamonds all around them, as this actually brings down the value of the watch despite how nice they look.

Gold is another item that usually goes up in value. If possible, stick to the higher grades of gold like 24k, as they give you a better return in the event you decide to sell it later. Diamonds lose value as soon as you walk out of the store, unless it's a very special quality diamond. Diamonds are a girl's best friend, and so is debt accumulation. Diamond companies have done a good job of marketing diamonds as a means of a man expressing his love for a woman. If you want to go into debt as a way to express your love for someone then by all means knock yourself out, but I just want you to know that if, for whatever reason, you decide to sell that diamond later on, you'll likely get nowhere near what you paid for it.

There's nothing better than getting some new threads to wear to the club, or any social event for that matter, but buying nice clothes should be about comfort and not brand. Most expensive clothing just feels better and fits better. I used the word most because some brands only rely on brand name and not the quality of material as a reason for the high pricing.

Avoid trendy clothing at all cost—in style one season, out of style the next. When you buy clothing for material comfort instead of logos, those clothes never go out of style. I have $500 cashmere sweaters, and they'll be in style ten years from now. Better material also has lasting power, as they hold up better over time. No matter the purchase, if you decide to reward yourself from time to time, just make sure it's kept to a minimum of your income, as overdoing it will slow your progress toward achieving financial freedom.

Passive Income Ideas

There are several ways you can generate passive income. I've already discussed real estate, stocks, and bonds ad nauseam, so right now, I would like to discuss other ideas to create passive income.

Let's say, for example, that you have a passion for comedy. You can't generate passive income touring the country doing standup, so how would you go about generating passive income as a comedian? The answer is to record one of your performances and sell it on a pay per view basis—sort of like what Netflix has done with several comedians. This is a much more attractive way to go about your money instead of just making money when you're performing now, you're making money while you sleep.

This is only possible, however, after you've gone through the process of creating a following via social media. You could also just create a following from performing. There are no shortcuts to success, so before I go any further, let me tell you none of the things I'm about to outline are possible without first going through the process of building a loyal clientele base or social media following, as I've already outlined how to build that following earlier in the book.

Let's say you have a passion for carpentry. How would you go about making passive income in this area? There are several ways to generate passive income in a skill like carpentry. For one, you could hire employees to work for you, but of course you have to have the clientele for this. You could also create a course or program teaching basic carpentry or something to that effect. It sounds daunting, but this is how entrepreneurs think; they think big.

Once again, creating that course or program would do you hardly any good if you didn't have some major financial backing or a social media following. If you have a business idea you're thinking of, I suggest you start building a social media following now, because it can take you years to build this following, but that's fine because it might take you years to figure out exactly the product you want to produce.

Now, I know some are reading this right now saying to themselves, “Who this guy kidding with his build a social media following?” And what I say to those individuals is if I’ve done it, you can too. What makes me better than you? What I’ve learned in my nearly forty years of living is that it’s much easier for people to complain and make excuses than to take action.

Whether you’re offering a product or a service, you need some type of exposure, and if you don’t have the capital for radio or TV ads, then your only recourse is social media. No matter what skill you have, if you want to generate passive income with that skill, the goal has to be to either hire employees to work for you, or to somehow create a product that teaches that skill in some kind of capacity.

Self-help products like this book are always in demand. It could be a course, book, or program. It doesn’t have to be something that tries to turn the average Joe into the greatest carpenter or tile layer in the history of the world, but if it can help people with very basic, around-the-house needs, you might have yourself a best seller. It doesn’t matter if this product has been created a million times, as no one holds the rights to teaching a skill.

There are thousands of financial and dating books, but that didn’t discourage me from writing my own books. There’s a customer born every second, and instead of buying those other self-help books, maybe they’ll buy mine instead.

Another thing to consider is that everyone always has a slightly different philosophy to pretty much anything we do in life. I’m quite sure I’ve said things in this book that you don’t 100 percent agree with. This is why creating your own following is pivotal. There’s always a different perspective you can bring to the conversation.

Obviously, if you have a product like clothing, you want to build it to where you can hire employees to handle the delivery process, or there are some online stores that do it for you. The key, however, is to build enough of a clientele base where it's worth paying someone to handle the shipping for you.

If It Was Easy, Everyone Would Be Doing It

Right now, I know the average person reading this is probably rolling their eyes at me thinking to themselves, "Who is this guy kidding?" First, I should get a marketable skill or education, then he wants me to get a job and live well below my means, all in an effort to save money, so I can invest. All the while I'm building a social media following, so I have an audience to sell to once I start my own business.

While all of this happened to be true. My question to you would be if it was easy, don't you think everyone would be doing it? The blueprint that I've laid out to success is not meant to be an easy one. That's the point. It's a reason being wealthy is so attractive to us all, and that's because it's not easily attainable. Getting abs is not an easy task for the vast majority of the population and, therefore, it's highly coveted.

Let me add in the fact that this will in all likelihood require many years of hard work and sacrifice to accomplish, but please understand that those sacrifices just make it that more enjoyable once you've accomplished it.

When I was a bouncer at a club in Manhattan, there was this rich kid who was the relative of a very rich family. I witnessed him, with my own eyes, tearing up hundred-dollar bills. Why would someone be tearing hundred dollar bills up? It's called inheritance and not having to work for the money he was wasting. See, had he been the one who had to sacrifice to accumulate that wealth, he wouldn't be tearing it up. He didn't have to sacrifice to build that family's wealth.

A little hard work and sacrifice never killed anyone, so be prepared to work your butt off, and don't expect riches overnight.

Nothing Beats a Quality Product

Let me be emphatically clear when I say, *nothing beats a good product*! Word of mouth will always be your best bet to build your business. You can try to create as many catchy ads promoting your business, but if your product isn't any good, it will not succeed, period.

Human beings have this uncanny ability—or should I say inability—to keep things to themselves. Just think to yourself for a second, whenever you've encountered a product during your lifetime, whether good or bad, how often have you not told anyone else about your experience with that particular product? Not often, huh, particularly when it was a good experience?

This should be an indicator to you that trying to create a subpar product or service and hoping to gain success with that lackluster product is very futile. For instance, I'm hoping you have a very positive effect from reading this book. Therefore, you tell other individuals about it, encouraging them to buy.

This doesn't even take into account the effect of positive and negative reviews one might leave. Reviews are a way of doing business now, and I can surely guess that I'm not the only one who does their due diligence before buying a product by reading reviews. Whenever I'm deciding on a book, restaurant, club etc. I always take into account what the majority of reviews are indicating. I do this because I'm well aware that it's nearly impossible for every consumer or customer to have a positive experience.

We live in an era where people are butthurt about almost everything imaginable. A restaurant not rolling out the red carpet for some customers, or putting six cubes of ice in their drink instead of five, these days leads to a negative review on Yelp, unfortunately, so I wouldn't base my decision entirely on a couple of bad reviews, but if it's loaded with mostly bad reviews, then I'm simply not going to reward that company's bad customer service with my hard earned money.

Don't spend most of your time centered around marketing and strategizing on how to get potential customers to buy your product or service. Don't get me wrong; marketing definitely plays an important part in being successful, but just make sure you're putting that same amount of time and energy, if not more, into creating a great product.

As the old saying goes, a great product sells itself. Being a YouTuber myself, I can tell you firsthand that there are multiple channels with better editing, graphics, thumbnails, etc. You name it, they have it, but a lot of them are missing one major piece: delivery and results.

Guys listen to the advice I give and have success applying it in their everyday life. Therefore they tell their friends about my channel, thus creating a snowball effect. This snowball effect allows me the ability to just create more content without me having to strategize on how to grow my channel, and you won't either if you create a tried and tested product.

Careers to Pursue

Finding your purpose in life is not something that just comes overnight, more times than not. Although I discovered my passion at in my early twenties, I didn't know how I could make a living at it until my midthirties.

Being a life coach for over a couple of years now, I can tell you firsthand that there are a lot of people who have this same problem or even worse, haven't even discovered their passion in life.

As I've mentioned earlier if you haven't discovered your passion, you may want to consider stepping out of your comfort zone and try different things. Even so, it still may take you several years to discover your passion, so I have some fields you may consider until then.

We all would love the opportunity to do what we love for a living, but the facts of the matter are that we also have bills and responsibilities. You can't expect Mom and Dad to be OK with you wandering through life, waiting to find your purpose in life, all the while sleeping in their basement.

Without a shadow of a doubt, the medical field is a good field to pursue a career in. You can never pick up a wanted ad without seeing tons of jobs available. Unfortunately, people will always get sick, and as long as people get sick, there will be jobs available.

Truck driving is another job that's always available and pays pretty well. I wouldn't even think of making truck driving a career as the mere thought of driving trucks cross country for extended periods depresses me. I would, however, make a plan to save my money for a couple of years all the while trying to find my passion in life. Driving trucks is one of those jobs that's always available, due to the high turnover rate from truck driving burnout, undoubtedly.

We're living in a world that's getting more technical everyday so a job that deals with technology is surely on the right path. Information technology comes to mind.

Law enforcement or joining the fire department are pretty good fields to pursue if you haven't discovered your passion in life. Apart from a situation where your city has to make cuts to the city budget like during the Great Recession, it's a pretty safe and reliable career to pursue.

Notice I said career. That's because these two fields have promotional opportunities within the department with great fringe benefits and great pension retirement.

You can't go wrong with acquiring a skill or trade. This skill or trade could be (but not limited to) electrician, plumber, welder, auto mechanic, etc. These skills pay fairly well and should allow you to save money, as long as you live below your means, in the event you discover your passion in life and want to make a career change.

Enjoy the Fruits of Your Labor

Everyone has different reasons for wanting to accomplish success, so I'll just state what my prime motivating factor was. My motivating factor was not to buy a ton of luxury items, although I do indulge every now and then. It wasn't so I could wake up in a hammock on the beach every day either, as I knew this would get old to me very quickly. The driving force behind me wanting to become successful through creating multiple streams of passive income was simple: I wanted to live life on my terms.

When I'm referencing living life on my terms, I'm referring to the ability to make my own schedule and the ability to enjoy any activity within reason, and by within reason, I simply mean that renting a yacht for a week might be a little out of my budget. But that's something that doesn't interest me anyway, but an international trip does.

While I understand why some individuals have a need or want to become a billionaire, that really isn't my goal. I want peace and happiness in my life. Most billionaires spend most of their life working themselves to the bone, all for the title of billionaire. Some never even allow themselves a chance to enjoy their money. Now don't misunderstand me; I'll be working until the day I die, because not having something meaningful to do would get old to me very quickly.

But I won't be working eighty-hour weeks either. For workaholics who never stop to smell the roses, it's usually the children or relatives who get to enjoy the money after they've passed away. I'm a stop-and-smell-the-roses type of guy, after I've accomplished my goals, of course.

If you don't have any money in the bank, and you haven't created any streams of passive income, you should not be stopping to smell anything. You should be full throttle into creating the life you want. But if you've busted your behind for several years and through hard work and determination, you've gotten your life to a point where you can kick back, you should take advantage of it, even if you're doing something you're passionate about. Life is about balance and too much of anything is never good.

When to Retire

Complete retirement isn't something I'm interested in, but there does come a point where you want to slow down a bit.

Retirement is something that most individuals never concern themselves with because we live in the YOLO (you only live once) era. This means you live life like every day is your last. That might be a little hyperbole, but you get what I'm saying. People live this YOLO lifestyle, all the while waiting and hoping for Uncle Sam to take care of them when they get old.

A good rule of thumb in life is that you should never depend on anything or anyone. This is why we diversify our investments. You never want to put all your eggs in one basket. The Medicare system is on life support, and it just isn't wise to depend on a government that goes deeper into debt every year.

Let me introduce you to the Trinity study. The Trinity study is a study that bought about the 4 percent rule for retirement. Basically, it's saying that you need to have twenty-five times your yearly living expenses saved up and creating passive income.

Take me for instance. I could maintain my lifestyle in New York without having to downgrade my lifestyle with approximately $72,000 a year. That's $6,000 a month that I've calculated for my total living expenses. I could bring it down if I moved down south or didn't date as much, but I don't want to live like a hermit when I retire. I want to be able to still enjoy my life.

With that being said, this would mean that I need approximately $1.8 million invested in the stock market, which would make me about $72,000 or 4 percent. The 4 percent is what you're left with after you've accounted for inflation.

The stock market historically has given back about a 7 percent return over time. Some people say more, but I think it's smart to always go with the smallest number. If it's more, then fine; that can just be icing on the cake, but you should always use a worst-case scenario when doing these types of calculations, in my opinion.

Remember, you have some years better than others, but over time it's been about 7 percent. You would probably make a little more if you invested in real estate, but I think it's smart to use the lesser of the two. This means that I could maintain my lifestyle without ever touching my principle of $1.8 million. Quite frankly, $72,000 is a lot to live on, but it isn't needed in the US for pretty much anyone living outside of New York or California, so I'll use a much more realistic example.

Let's assume you could maintain your lifestyle on $30,000 a year. This would mean that you need to have about $750,000 saved, creating passive income for you. From $750,000, 4 percent would generate enough income if invested properly to maintain your lifestyle without having to downgrade. Let's say you're one of the individuals whose absolutely terrified to invest your money and just prefers to just save your money in a savings account that offers interest rates that keep up with inflation, and you decided to retire at sixty-five years old and just live off $30,000 a year until your death.

Your savings of $750,000 would last you approximately twenty-five years. I guess theoretically it could be done coupled with your social security benefits. What if you're one of the lucky or—depending on perspective—unlucky ones who lives to 100 years of age? That would mean you would have to live on just your social security income at the age of ninety.

Another thing to consider is it's very hard for the average person to accumulate $750,000 without investing their money. Without a shadow of doubt, investing is the only viable solution to achieving financial freedom. The last scenario is probably a far stretch, but I just wanted to look at every angle nonetheless.

Loaning Money Once Becoming Successful

Once you've accomplished any semblance of success, be prepared for family and friends to come with their hands out looking for a handout. Sad to say, but this is the entitlement world we live in, and if you don't give it to them, you're the bad guy.

The love of money is the root of all evil, as the saying goes, and be prepared to be outcast from loved ones if you're not overly generous with your finances. The problem isn't giving anyone anything, but once you've made the mental shift from consumer to seller, you never look at money the same way again. There was once upon a time when I had a consumer's mind-set that whenever I had money, I looked at it as something to be spent on whatever I liked.

Now, I look at money totally differently, since acquiring an entrepreneurial mind-set. Therefore, I'm always looking for ways to use my money to create more money. Also, once you've escaped the victim mentality—and by victim mentality, I'm referring to blaming *the man* for my shortcomings—you realize that if anyone got off their behinds, they could change their life around. Before, I would've probably felt sorry for them, since everything was *the man's* fault.

Be that as it may, you're still going to encounter lazy, selfish, jealous loved ones, so how should you handle them? All of our family dynamics are different, as I know some families might be a lot closer than my family, so I'll just tell you how I handle when family and friends ask me for money.

If it's someone I felt like would help me out if I was in a time of need, I would do it. If it was someone who I felt would help me out if I needed it, but they weren't trying to progress, I wouldn't, due to the fact I would then become their enabler. Enabling is the biggest issue when it comes to helping loved ones.

As I've said earlier, the biggest thing I want to give my family is a shift in mentality, not financial gain. I want them to develop the same mind-set I've developed and create their own financial freedom. What if a family member needs a large sum of money, and you're pretty sure they would never be able to pay you back? Well, in a situation like this, it's going to depend on the tightness of the relationship and the willingness on your part to just take that loan as a loss.

If you're expecting someone who makes $25,000 a year to pay you back that $5,000 loan you gave them for whatever reason, you're dreaming. You may get some back, but it's likely that even with a large tax refund, they won't want to pay you back. At the end of the day, you're not obligated to give anyone anything, including family members, so part of becoming financial and mentally free is accepting that everyone is not going to like you. If you need every family member or friend to love you, you'll never be free mentally.

As a successful entrepreneur, you're going to have to make some very tough decisions along the way, whether it's cutting cost by laying off employees, or having to tell your only sibling no on a loan they ask you for.

No one said the road to becoming financially and mentally free would be a walk in the park. It's a very long road that requires shedding yourself of any and all dead weight along the way.

Compound Interest

Compound interest is perhaps the greatest tool used to create wealth. The great Albert Einstein referred to it as the 8th wonder of the world. He also stated, "He who understands it, earns it...he who doesn't...pays it." That statement, in simpler terms, means your money is earning interest by way of investments, or you're probably in debt paying interest.

The rich take advantage of compounding interest by making smart investments, while poor people go into debt to keep up with the Joneses and end up paying interest. I know you're probably wondering "how does my money compound?"

Let's assume you have $1,000 in the bank, and let's assume you have it in a savings account that offers 2 percent interest rates. When the bank calculates your interest payments, not only will it apply the interest payment to your principle of $1,000 but now it will add 2 percent to your overall savings. For example, if the bank paid you 2 percent on your $1,000 and now you have $1,020. The next time the bank adds interest to your balance, it will add the 2 percent interest rate to the $1,020 you now have, not just your initial principle of $1,000.

That may seem small, but over time, small things add up. This is why it takes time to accumulate wealth. The rule of seventy-two is a formula used to determine how long it will take for your money to double. You take the number seventy-two and divide it by whatever your interest rate is. For instance, if you have that same $1,000 in the bank, and as before, you're earning a 2 percent interest rate. That means it would take you thirty-six years to double that $1,000. I know it's not a lot and would take an awfully long time, but that's why you have to invest as much money as possible.

If we used that same formula, and you had $20,000 in the stock market, and let's just assume you averaged 6 percent ROI, it would only take you twelve years to double that $20,000.

If you truly want to experience true financial freedom you have to take advantage of compounding interest. Ignorance of these types of things are what hindered many minority communities. I'm thirty-nine years old at the time of writing this book, and I had never heard of compound interest until I was about thirty-five years old.

Taxes

There are two things in this world that are guaranteed: death and taxes. Everyone understands the death part, but many disagree with the taxes part. While I, like many, don't like to pay taxes, I do understand the need for them.

There are plenty of terrorists around the world who are hell-bent on blowing America up. This requires us to have multiple federal agencies to disrupt their efforts. This is paid for by taxes. We sleep well at night because millions of criminals around the world are locked behind bars. This responsibility is held by correctional officers who are paid by—yes, you guessed it—taxes. The police, fire department, teachers, courts, probation officers are just some of the departments that are funded through taxes.

When you look at it that way, it makes you feel a lot better about paying taxes because just putting it bluntly, the country couldn't function without taxes. If you're an aspiring entrepreneur looking to start your business, you need to make sure you have business spending tracked properly. I ran into this issue when I started my first business. I was ignorant of bookkeeping, and therefore, doing my first year's taxes was very time consuming, having to scan through my credit card statements to find the items I had purchased for my business.

To avoid this same issue I had, you should have a credit or debit card that's only for business obligations. You should have separate bank accounts to avoid mixing your income. This protects you in the event of a legal liability. Although I did have separate checking accounts for my business and personal income, I would use my personal credit card to acquire the cash back benefits thus creating a mess when it came time to do my write-offs for taxes. I literally had to go through each credit card statement to find my write-offs.

To avoid this, just apply for a business credit card, and therefore, you can still enjoy the cash back benefits credit cards offer without causing a confusion when it's time to do your taxes. Anything you bought that was for your business is considered a write-off.

Don't blur the lines with expensive lunch dates with friends and try to pass this off as a write-off because you were all allegedly discussing business. Trying to pass something off like this would probably only trigger an audit.

When you sell a long-term investment—and by long-term, I'm referring to over a year—you can take advantage of what's called a capital gains tax. A capital gains tax is what allows a lot of rich people to pay less in tax than someone who makes considerably less. Let's say I have some Apple stock I've had over five years, valued at $500,000, and I've decided to sell my stock. Let's assume that out of that $500,000, $60,000 was profit from my initial investment. I would not pay the 25–30 percent as I would with earned income. I would only be required to pay 15 percent or 20 percent.

This doesn't just apply to stocks but any long-term investment like real estate, business, etc. In some cases, you can actually avoid paying any, depending on loopholes found by your accountant. These loopholes are why a certain politician doesn't want his taxes public.

This should only incentivize you more to invest your money. Not only do investments allow you to make passive income, but they also get taxed at a lower tax rate when you decide to sell them.

The government wants entrepreneurs creating jobs and thus offers a ton of tax benefits for those willing to take the chance and invest. No need in complaining about the rich avoiding taxes when they're just taking advantage of the tax breaks the government offers any of us.

How to Overcome Hard Times and Adversities

Life has many uncertainties, that's for sure. That's why I stress having an emergency fund so much throughout this book. I want you to invest your money so that you're able to create passive income, but only after you have a nice nest egg set in place.

The reason for this is because we all will experience highs and lows throughout our lifetime. No matter how healthy you are today, there's always a chance that you can be stricken with an unforeseen illness at any given time and place. No matter how good your financial situation is right now there's no guarantee on how good your business will be doing this time next year.

Hard times and adversities are brought on by not preparing for life's low points when times were better. If your hard times are a cause of you not having disposable income to save for a rainy day, then that too is a cause and effect of your life's decisions. At the end of the day, not having a skill or education that allows you to earn the kind of money that can be set aside for a rainy day, never mind investing, is a decision that you made and have to take responsibility for.

Maybe you have a skill or education that allows you to have disposable income to save, but you only consumed more liabilities thus preventing you from saving for a rainy day, which has to fall at your doorstep. You have to learn how to live below your means and not worry about what Michael, Jeffrey, and Sarah think of you. That's the proactive approach.

Here's the reactive approach. If you're already mired in a situation where you're going through hard times and adversities, you have to look at it as a learning experience, first and foremost.

Sad to say, but this is usually what it takes for a person to take saving money for a rainy day more serious, at least for me it was. I got fired from a machine operator job when I was in my early twenties. I lost my apartment and ended up having to move back home with my auntie. I'm not talking about three months after losing my job, I'm talking about the very next month, since I was living check to check. Now I was making decent money but nothing mind-blowing, so I'm not suggesting that I should've had a million dollars saved up, but I could have had at least three or four months if I would have simply saved $50 a week from each check.

If your adversities come from not saving your money, then simply accept it as a learning experience and know to do better next time. Even with me saying this, most of you are not going to take heed of this until you are actually put in the situation, and that's fine. Life is one big learning experience.

My family might not have taught me much in the way of financial education, but they did try to teach me to save my money for a rainy day. It went in one ear and right out the other. Experience has, and will always be, the best teacher. If your hard times and adversities are brought on by the lack of financial earning ability from not acquiring a marketable skill or education, then you should use this opportunity to improve your earning potential.

What's the point of just getting another lackluster paying job? This is what Albert Einstein was referring to when he defined insanity; doing the same thing over and over, expecting a different result is insane.

I'm well aware that you may be an adult with responsibilities, but that doesn't absolve you from the responsibility of improving your earning potential. This may require you to work a full-time job and taking classes on the side to acquire the knowledge you need to bring more value to the marketplace. This is the price you have to pay for not acquiring it when you were younger.

No one said overcoming hard times and adversities was going to be a cake walk. You can either bitch and moan about the situation you're in, or you can accept it as one of life's many challenges and be determined to come out on top.

Body Language

If you're planning on building a successful business, you need to know that your body language is going to play a major role in that.

The first thing a potential customer is going to notice about you is your clothing and body language. Your body language is an indication of your confidence. This is all subconscious, though, as most individuals don't actively seek out someone's confidence level. Most of human interaction is subconsciously done on a primal level. When you go up to a potential client or customer with the body language of an individual who lacks confidence, the message you send is that you don't wholeheartedly believe in your product or service.

This is why you see salesmen with high energy levels when trying to sell their product or service. That high energy and strong body language sends signals that they truly believe in the product they're selling. These confident body language signals can include upright body positioning: shoulders back, head up, eye contact, firm handshake, confident tone, etc.

Nonconfident body language usually consists of fidgeting body movements, head down, stuttering, rounded torso, etc.

Unfortunately, you can't fake true confidence, so what's the solution? The solution is to develop a product or service that you truly believe in. I advise this anyway, as a subpar product won't survive the test of time. Once the word gets out that your product isn't that good, it'll only fail long-term anyway. When you develop a strong product that you truly believe in, the confidence just comes naturally.

How to Make Friends

Networking is vital in creating a successful business, so knowing how to make these new friendships is critical for success. You can build a successful business without networking, but networking will open doors and make the path a lot smoother.

I teach guys how to master the ability to be alone, but that should only be something used if you have crappy negative friends. We humans are social creatures, so you shouldn't strive to be alone, but you shouldn't shy away from it, if need be.

As a life coach, I've been asked quite often how to make friends. Well, the answer is simple: the same way you meet someone of the opposite sex. You go up and introduce yourself.

The key to making friendships is to have things in common, the same way you would in dating. How would you go about meeting individuals with the same interests as you? By engaging in activities that you enjoy. If you love to roller-skate, then try making friends at the skating rink. If you love art, then try making friends at a museum.

This is the same advice I give individuals who are looking for love. I shouldn't say looking for love, as we all know you never find anything when you're looking for it, but rather, just enjoying your life, doing what you love to do, and if the person of your dreams just so happens to be there that day, then who knows.

It's called the law of attraction, and you should just let life come to you. There are so many parallels in our business and social lives that it's really strange at how familiar they are. Now, if you happen to see an individual you wouldn't mind making acquaintances with, then you should just go up and introduce yourself, but as in the dating world, it doesn't mean they're going to reciprocate your hospitality. Maybe they're not in the friend-making mood that day, or maybe they're the type to naturally have their guard up.

Whatever the case, just be prepared to not be welcomed with open arms every time you introduce yourself to someone. The key is to not let unfriendly individuals deter you from trying to make friends.

Sometimes, you may go through the hassle of exchanging numbers with someone, only to find out they were only being nice in the moment. Don't hound someone to be your friend. If they don't reciprocate the outreach, then they don't deserve your friendship anyway. What I've discovered in my life is that the older you get, the harder it gets to make new friends. This is probably due to the fact that most people are naturally more adherent to having their guards up as, sad to say, some people just aren't good-hearted individuals.

If you want to connect to others try engaging in different activities and hobbies. Become an interesting person and avoid being a homebody, unless you're building your empire. Make sure these individuals are on the same path as you, as people who aren't grinding like you will likely only bring jealousy or self-doubt.

I know making friends might not seem important when it comes to improving your financial situation, but I wholeheartedly disagree. A strong support system can go a tremendous way toward creating the life you want. And besides, life is just better when you have other like-minded individuals to share it with.

Most loners would argue that it's better to go at it alone, and that's ok if you truly enjoy being alone, but the fact of the matter is that most loners are really individuals who just lack social skills. Rather than improve this, they hide behind their shyness, awkwardness, or lack of social skills.

I believe that most people can develop the social life they want if they're willing to put the work in becoming more socially aware.

Controlling Your Emotions

Humans were blessed with the gift and the curse of having emotions. I say it's the gift and the curse because emotions are what gives us the ability to love, bond, and care for others, but on the other hand, these same emotions can work against you when your love isn't reciprocated or appreciated.

Not being in control of your emotions can have a devastating impact toward obtaining your goals. Falling in love with someone who doesn't deserve it can leave you in a state of hopelessness. I think we've all experienced that heartbreak, where we couldn't eat or sleep, and it impacted our lives in a negative capacity. Life would be so much easier if we had the ability to just not care about certain individuals who don't deserve our love, but unfortunately, we do—so what's the solution?

The answer is to never love anyone outside of close family members more than you love your purpose. This means that your purpose in life comes before any significant other. When we meet someone we really like, we slowly gravitate more of our time toward that individual and slowly away from our purpose in life. This is a mistake, because you're now making that individual more of a priority than your purpose. Nothing should come before your purpose, except for maybe close friends and family. Even that is probably a stretch.

Doing so ensures that you never get too invested into someone. Now if you're the unambitious type, then this won't matter, as your purpose in life is probably to find someone to love. Ambitious individuals aren't afraid to love, but it can't come at the expense of reaching our goals. There is a big difference.

Emotions come in other forms other than just falling in love. It also comes in the form of anger. We live in a world where, unfortunately, there are plenty of aggravating people, some who try to deliberately to get under our skin. You're not going to obtain the goals you're striving for if you're going to let certain individuals derail the process.

You should expect haters, as haters are only a sign of your success. Haters are par for the course, so you have to learn how to not let them get under your skin.

The thing that has worked wonders for me is to always remember consequences are a real thing. There was a pivotal moment in my life to help remind me of this. When I got fired from my job in my early twenties due to letting another employee get under my skin, it cost me everything. I had to move back in with my auntie, and I had to find another job. The job I had was a pretty decent job for my age, and it provided benefits. Every job after that paled in comparison.

This little life lesson would come in handy when I became a personal trainer in the city working for a big commercial gym. There was a manager with whom I didn't see eye to eye, and we didn't like one another. Had I not gone through that previous experience earlier in my life, I would have surely blown that opportunity because I'm not afraid to speak my mind.

While speaking your mind isn't necessarily a bad thing, there is a time and place for it. Had I let my emotions get the better of me, I would've lost the job that laid the building blocks for changing my life around.

I'm hoping from reading this that you don't have to actually go through losing everything before you think of the consequences of your actions. I know that experience is the best teacher, but I don't need to experience first-degree burns before I understand that playing with fire is dangerous.

Overcoming emotional spending has helped me tremendously because I no longer need to buy things to make me feel better, thanks to finding my purpose in life. When you have no purpose in life, you tend to rely on frivolous things like spending to pass time and to make you feel better about yourself. News flash: those Gucci shoes might make you feel better for a short period of time, but when the novelty wears off, you'll be wondering why you spent $800 for a pair of shoes when you're already in debt.

Pursuing your purpose is very time consuming, and you don't have that void to fill in your life. That void we experience in life leads us to looking for love, engaging in expensive habits like gambling and shopping, all in an effort to fill our spare time with. Wouldn't that spare time be better suited doing something that creates money instead of depleting your bank account?

Once you learn how to master your emotions, you control your destiny because no longer are you burdened with the negative effects that emotions cause.

How to Handle Insecurities

Dealing with insecurities is one of the biggest detriments you will have to overcome on your way to success. No matter how perfect someone seems, we all have our insecurities we have to deal with on a day-to-day basis. Sometimes these insecurities manifest in our heads, and we make them bigger than what they actually are.

Once you start to think something is an issue, you start to project those insecurities more because that's how our minds work. If you think it, then so it shall be.

I overcame my insecurities by realizing that no one's perfect. Everyone has a flaw in some sort of way. These flaws are what make us unique and different from everyone else. You can either accept your insecurities and be grateful for what you have, rather than complaining you're not perfect, or you hide from your insecurities and let them control you during every interaction throughout your life.

Some men are comfortable being short, while others complain they're not tall enough. What I would tell the short men who complain about their height is that it could've been worse. You could've been born unable to walk.

I've been told and mocked repeatedly throughout my life that I don't speak well. When someone tries to bring this to my attention, I'm thinking to myself, "At least I can speak at all." There are mutes in the world unable to mutter one word.

Let's just be honest about things for a second. Most individuals use insecurities as an excuse to explain their failure or lack of effort in life. Short men want to use their height as an excuse as to why they can't attract women, while there are plenty of short men with women. I could use my speech inadequacies as an excuse to why I couldn't sell at the gym or make quality YouTube videos. I chose to overcome my speech inadequacies and become one of the most popular Youtubers out there. I think I did a very good job of that.

My mind-set behind all of this is that they can either accept my flaws and all, or not. You have to apply the same thought toward your insecurities, everyone can accept you as-is, or they can choose not to. More times than not, whatever you're insecure about, most people probably don't even notice, and it's just a figment of your imagination. You can't expect people to accept your inadequacies if you don't.

Karma

Creating wealth is fun but sharing your wealth with the less fortunate is even more fun. While I believe most of us who are able-bodied are given the same opportunities to create wealth with hard work, I do believe there are charities worthwhile to share your wealth with, especially children's charities and charities dealing with disabilities.

This is what I classify as special population, and these are the type of charities I recommend. Even able-bodied individuals can fall to circumstances. You hear all the time how people lost everything in a house fire and didn't have insurance, or they got laid off from their job.

We already know most people don't have an adequate savings due to low wages and or bad spending habits. I was victim to this a couple times in my life and believe that people deserve help despite ignorance.

That's the reason I'm writing this book, to educate individuals who might not understand how wealth is created, as I didn't know just six short years ago. What I've learned in my nearly forty years of living is that when you have a giving heart, it comes back to you tenfold. You should give from your heart and not expect some sort of good karma to come back your way.

But I can't help but notice that every time I've done a good deed in my life, karma has come back and blessed me tenfold. When you do good things in life, good luck follows you, and when you do bad things in life, bad luck follows you. Helping the less fortunate also gives you a good feeling inside of doing something that's greater than you.

This probably explains why some billionaires choose to donate most of their money before their passing—notably, John D. Rockefeller and Andrew Carnegie. I'm quite sure a small part of that is to ensure their legacy lives on long after their passing, but I know it also has to be such a great feeling helping the less fortunate.

You reap what you sow. If you plant bad seeds in life, they'll come back to bite you in the end. That's why being a good person with a giving heart is a much better lifestyle to live.

Get-Rich-Quick Schemes

You see them everywhere. We live in a world where everyone wants something for nothing. This holds true in the financial and fitness worlds, as I've experienced both firsthand.

Being a personal trainer for several years, and just being in the fitness world in general, has given me a firsthand account of how people try to find everything possible to cut corners. This is why, at night, you see different fitness infomercials, promising you a six-pack without changing your diet. They purposely take advantage of people's naive nature and laziness to make millions.

Every week there's another fad diet promising fast results. Why not just tell people the truth, that losing weight takes a long time with persistence and dedication? Because people wouldn't buy their product. Most people are lazy and impatient.

You see the same thing going on with these fast-talking, get-rich-overnight scheme guys. More times than not, the program they're selling can get you rich, but the timeline they promise is most times very unrealistic. Sometimes the product they're selling is a complete farce.

Let me make this abundantly clear right now: losing weight is the action of eating in a calorie deficit for an extended period of time. A calorie deficit means you're eating fewer calories than you need to maintain your body weight. The type of diet doesn't matter as long as you're in a calorie deficit. Of course, some diets are healthier than others, but I'm speaking on a purely body-weight comparison.

Getting rich doesn't happen overnight unless you win the lottery or get an inheritance; otherwise it's going to take time. Even the people you see in the entertainment industry who seemingly struck it rich overnight have usually been honing their craft for several years before finally striking gold.

We've all seen the overnight sensation that struck it rich by putting out a hit song. What you don't hear about is the years they spent working on their craft before finally creating a hit. As the old saying goes, it took me several years to become an overnight success.

Nobody sees the grind you put in. They only see the shine at the end of the rainbow. Do not become a victim of a fad exercise equipment, diets, or get rich scheme. People are only trying to profit from your laziness. The only one that's going to get rich quick is them.

Value Your Time

When I watched celebrities with maids, drivers, personal assistants, chefs, etc. I would think they had these individuals so they could just be lazy. Once I became an entrepreneur, I quickly realized why they had these individuals helping them. Their time is better spent doing what they do for a living than cleaning their homes and cooking meals. It's much more productive for them to focus on their profession and to just pay someone to do the other things they need done.

This is called valuing your time. When I first became a life and dating coach, I quickly realized it was much more productive to spend my time writing books than to be doing Skype sessions and training sessions all day. This forced me to raise my Skype session prices because my time was better spent doing something that would create passive income, as opposed to trading time for money.

If your goal is to obtain financial freedom, you might have to sacrifice some money on the front end to focus on creating passive income. It's hard to do initially, because you're giving up guaranteed money, but it's what needed to create these streams of income. My goal is to write at least one book—perhaps even two books—a year. There's no way I could accomplish this if I was doing Skype sessions all night and training clients in the morning.

You have to think to yourself what's better in the long term? If you want to achieve financial freedom, you have to rid yourself of trading time for money. It's shortsighted. If you're engaging in activities that don't make money while you're sleeping, then you're on the wrong path.

All this should be done once you've gotten a skill and financial stability, of course. Don't try to put the cart before the horse. You're going to have to trade time for money initially. If you can't figure out how to monetize your passion, then you can always just use your active income to invest in stocks and real estate to create passive income.

The perfect situation would be for you to monetize your passion in life, then buy real estate and stocks.

We all can achieve financial freedom if we employ a little self-restraint and long-term thinking.

Printed in Great Britain
by Amazon

61347961R00133